SMOOTH STONES

Bringing Down the Giant Questions of Apologetics

Joe Coffey
Cruciform Press | Released June, 2011

To my wife, Karen, whose love and grace inspire me
daily. To my children Jeremy, Rachel, and Rebecca,
who continue to fill my life with joy. To my mom
and dad, who first taught me to love Jesus with both
my heart and my mind.
– Joe Coffey

CruciformPress

"What a thrill for me to see Joe Coffey, a graduate of our first Centurions Program class, apply the biblical worldview principles we teach at BreakPoint and the Colson Center.

"In this marvelous little book, *Smooth Stones: Bringing Down the Giant Questions of Aplogetics*, Joe simply and succinctly lays out the tenets of the Christian faith within the context of the four key life and worldview questions.

"This is an excellent resource for Christians and non-Christians alike who are seeking the Truth."

Chuck Colson
Founder of Prison Fellowship and the
Colson Center for Christian Worldview

"Most books on apologetics are too long, too deep, and too complicated. This book has none of these defects. Like its title, it is like a smooth stone from David's apologetic sling directed right to the mind of an enquiring reader."

Norman L. Geisler
Distinguished Professor of Apologetics
Veritas Evangelical Seminary, Murrieta, CA

Table of Contents

Print ISBN: 978-1-936760-20-6
ePub ISBN: 978-1-936760-21-3
Mobipocket ISBN: 978-1-936760-22-0

CruciformPress.com
something new in Christian publishing

email: info@CruciformPress.com
Facebook: http://on.fb.me/Cruciform
Twitter: @CruciformPress
Newsletter: http://bit.ly/CruciformNL

INTRODUCTION

It was just another article in the *New York Times*, but it spoke volumes to me.[1] Journalist Nicholas Kristof was concerned to find that Americans were three times more likely to believe in the Virgin Birth of Jesus than in evolution. To Kristof, this meant Christians were becoming less intellectual and more mystical, resulting in "a gulf, not only between America and the rest of the industrialized world, but a growing split at home as well." Kristof's bias came through loud and clear: "Despite the lack of scientific and historical evidence, and despite the doubts of biblical scholars, America is so pious that not only do 91 percent of Christians say they believe in the Virgin Birth, but so do an astonishing 47 percent of us non-Christians."

He went on to say, "I'm not denigrating anyone's beliefs, but mostly I'm troubled by the way the great intellectual traditions of Catholic and Protestant churches alike are withering, leaving the scholarly and religious worlds increasingly antagonistic."

Kristof concluded with this sentence: "The heart is a wonderful organ, but so is the brain."

Check Your Brain at the Door?

Why did I write *Smooth Stones*? There are two reasons. The first is there are so many people like Mr. Kristof— people who think believing in Christianity means you have to take your brain and put it on a shelf and simply trust with blind faith, against all odds, against all evidence, the way a child believes in Santa Claus or the Tooth Fairy. I think nothing could be further from the truth.

The second reason is that every two or three years, a new book intended to undermine Christianity will become a bestseller and shake the faith of many to the core. They'll say, "You know, I'm not sure anymore if what I believe is really true." And yet the arguments in these books, although well written, are typically not compelling.

In the Sermon on the Mount, Jesus likened our faith to a house built on a foundation.[2] If we build our house on a foundation of sand, when storms come and the winds of doubt blow, our house will fall. But if we build our house on a solid foundation, when storms come and doubts arise, our house will stand.

What I want to do in these pages is to inspect our foundation so we know *why* we believe what we believe. We will explore six issues: the existence of God, the challenges of modern science, the validity of the Bible, the question of evil and suffering, the similarities of other religions, and the evidence for the claims of Jesus. I think we will discover that the Christian faith is built on a tremendous amount of credible evidence. Christians have no reason to check their brains at the door.

A Word for Skeptics

If you find yourself reading this book even though you don't believe in God, the Bible, Jesus, or Christianity, I hope you will read it all the way to the end. It's a short book, so that shouldn't be a problem. I also hope you will weigh all the evidence with an open mind.

But I have another hope. Call it a request. Begin to read the Bible. I suggest you start with the Gospel of John.

Why would I ask someone who doesn't believe the Bible to read it anyway? Jesus told a story where an unbelieving man dies and immediately wishes he would have believed.[3] The man wants someone to go back and warn his brothers. He cries out (I'm paraphrasing here), "Please send somebody back from the dead so my brothers will see and understand." "They have the Bible," is the reply he gets. So the man basically says, "That's not enough. They need someone to come back from the dead." The last point Jesus makes in the story is to say that if people won't believe the Bible, neither will they believe if someone comes back from the dead and tries to tell them.

That's why I want you to read the Bible. It is the source for all God declares to be true. The time to read and understand and apply it is now—while we are alive.

I will cover the reasons you can trust the Bible as authentic and true in chapter three. But first let's look into the reasons to believe God even exists at all.

One
IS THERE A GOD?

In this world, God is known only by faith. So even though there are plenty of good reasons to believe—and I will present many of them in this little book—there is a sense in which no one can *prove* the existence of God.

In the same way, people who argue against the existence of God also have reasons for what they believe. But they cannot *disprove* God's existence any more than Christians can prove it. Believing in God or disbelieving—either one involves a degree of faith.

But it's interesting: I have found that nearly everyone who sides against God's existence, whether hard-core atheist or basic agnostic, has a disconnect. They may not believe God is there, yet they have these persistent internal moral convictions that people should *do* certain things and absolutely *not* do other things. In my discussions with unbelievers, exposing this and talking about it as an inconsistency has proven extremely helpful to them. So let's spend a few minutes on that topic. Then, at the end of this chapter, I will present the first category of evidence for the existence of God.

The Four Questions of Existence

The inconsistency, or flaw in logic, referred to above is best seen in light of what I'm calling The Four Questions of Existence.

1. The question of origin:
   Where did I come from?
2. The question of destiny:
   Where am I going?
3. The question of purpose:
   Why am I here?
4. The question of morality:
   How shall I live?

There are many varieties of answers. But here's the key point. The answers are linked—they are interdependent. No matter what answers you give, they have to be consistent with one another. Otherwise one's intellectual integrity falls apart. Your answer to *where you are going* depends on your answer to *where you came from*. And your answer to *why you are here* depends on your answer to *where you came from* and *where you are going*, and so forth. All four answers must stack like building blocks or else they will contradict one another and result in an unsupportable belief system.

We'll come back to this concept in a minute. But first, let's compare and contrast the way believers and unbelievers answer the four questions.

The Atheist/Agnostic Dilemma

Bible-believing Christians would answer The Four Questions of Existence more or less like this:

1. *Where did I come from?*
   From the hand of God, my Creator.
2. *Where am I going?*
   To heaven or hell for all of eternity.
3. *Why am I here?*
   To glorify and enjoy God.
4. *How shall I live?*
   The way God wants me to live; he is Lord.

Contrast those answers with the ones a student might get in a typical American high school. (I'm going to paint the picture a little starkly here to make my point.)

Question One: Origin. The student raises his hand in class and says, "I have a question. Where did I come from?"

"Well," the teacher might say, "according to one view of evolution, you came from a series of random mutations. You are an accident of nature. Some people think there may be a design behind that process, but it's hard to know that for sure. I think it's just a long series of mutations in which the strongest or best survive."

Question Two: Destiny. Then the student would say, "Hmm. Well, then, where am I going?" The answer to the second question, since it follows from the first question, must be, "If you are a series of mutations, and life is all about survival of the fittest, then when you die your body will fuel the organisms that come after you."

That's when the class clown jumps in and says, "He means you're food for worms, dude! Get used to it."

So the teacher adds, "Well, we definitely know what happens to the body, but some people say you also have a soul and that it lives on—happy if you were good, maybe unhappy if you were bad. Nobody really knows, and after all, that's not a question that can be examined scientifically."

Question Three: Purpose. The third question the young man would ask is, "Okay. Then why am I here?"

That's a tough one. Many unbelieving philosophers would answer by saying you have to take an *existential leap*—you have to create your own purpose. Maybe your purpose is to reproduce, or to make the world a better place, or to get all the pleasure you can, or to run for President. It's totally up to you.

So the teacher who believes that life came from mutations, and that after death we essentially just enrich the soil, would likely say something like this: "You are here to live a good life as a good citizen while enjoying yourself as much as you can." Interesting answer, isn't it? The second part, about just enjoying yourself, follows perfectly from the first two Questions of Existence, but where does the "live as a good citizen" stuff come from? More on that in a minute.

Question Four: Morality. Then, of course, the student's last question would be: "If that's true, then how shall I live?"

And the only answer consistent with the other three is essentially that *you should live however you want and do whatever you want.* But that won't be what the teacher actually says. He or she will have to civilize the answer a little, so it's not so brutal. So it might go something like, "Reach deep inside yourself and find an inner strength, and live out what is inside of you to do. Get a good enough education so that you can afford what you want and then try to do as much good as you want to do."

Insist on Consistency

It's no wonder America is so confused. Our atheist and agnostic friends typically answer questions one and two with reference to a particular view of science and reason and logic. Think Spock from Star Trek. In this view, God is just not allowed into the picture in any serious way. But when they get to questions three and four they feel compelled to introduce ideas about right and wrong, and good and bad, and loving people, and being good citizens. Really? Why? How does that follow from your answers to questions one and two? It doesn't. But we all know in our gut that if you answer questions three and four consistent with the answers I gave above for questions one and two, our world would come apart at the seams. So questions three and four get answered differently, and intellectual integrity comes apart at the seams instead.

In view of this, atheists and agnostics should choose their neighborhoods carefully—they may wind up in a place where some people think it's right to love your neighbor and others think it's fine to eat your neighbor. [4] Both are logical conclusions based on consistent answers to the atheist/agnostic view of The Four Questions of Existence.

Internal Evidence for the Existence of God

When the Bible tells us that God has placed eternity in the hearts of men,[5] it means he has woven into our very being an awareness of a reality beyond the material world. The nature of God himself is eternal. So we can expect to find evidence for God's existence within our very souls. This is what I call internal evidence. External evidence is found outside ourselves using the tool of science. I will cover that in chapter two.

In the remainder of this chapter I will present three exhibits of internal evidence: The Universal Concept, The Law of Human Nature, and the tendency toward Better Mental Health.

The Universal Concept

Every civilization that has ever existed on this planet has had a "God concept" as part of its core—from the Stone Age all the way to the present time. In that sense, belief in God is universal.

Take the culture here in the United States. Estimates are that between 86 and 96 percent of Americans believe in God.[6] In his book *God: The Evidence,* Patrick Glynn says people are wired for prayer, and in America, 90 percent of women and 85 percent of men say they pray daily. Even more amazing, of the 13 percent of Americans who describe themselves as atheists, one in five report they pray every day![7]

Human beings have an appetite for God. It's built in. And appetites always have a corresponding reality. I think it is safe to assume that our predominant tendency to some kind of belief in God is the result of an inner spiritual hunger—a hunger to know and relate to and commune with our Creator.

We do not hunger for that which does not exist. We hunger for food, or for knowledge, or for beauty, or for love, and those things *exist*. We can *imagine* something that doesn't exist. We can imagine a world where we could hear the color orange—we just don't long for it. We don't have an appetite for it. We don't write songs about it. We hunger for things that have a corresponding reality.

What is the corresponding reality for the worldwide spiritual hunger for God? The hunger that cuts across every culture, every people group, and every language for every civilization that has ever existed on the face of the earth?

The corresponding reality is God. For God has placed eternity in the hearts of men.

The Law of Human Nature

C. S. Lewis describes "our innate sense of right and wrong" in his book *Mere Christianity*.[8] Lewis says that a basic law, an overarching ethic of a sense of fairness, seems embedded in every human being. You can call it a sense of justice. It is something we all recognize. If you want to test this hypothesis, find a place where people line up, like the grocery store. Take your stuff and then just cut into the front of the line. No matter what the people behind you believe, they will all communicate the same thing—that what you are doing is unfair. They'll say, "Wait a minute! You can't do that!" Everybody knows it is wrong, because we have this overarching ethic, a hard-wired understanding of what is right and what is wrong.

At the Nuremberg trials after World War II, when the Allies tried the Nazis for war crimes against humanity, they didn't charge them with crimes against the law of Germany. What they said was, "You knew better, every human being knows better—you knew what you were doing was wrong." They convicted the Nazis on the basis of this overarching ethic that all human beings recognize deep in their own hearts as true.

Where does that kind of logic come from? God has placed eternity in the hearts of men.

Better Mental Health

Sigmund Freud was not a fan of religion. He thought belief in God was a sign of a mental disorder, something he called Universal Obsessional Neurosis. He said God does not exist, and to truly believe in something that does not exist and to live by that belief is to break from reality—an illness that needs to be cured.

In one sense, Freud was right. If a person breaks from reality and believes in something that doesn't exist, that belief will soon prove unhealthy—it will have a negative impact on his or her life. Let's say I believe Martians are hiding in the walls of my house. At first, I merely hear noises, but as time goes on I will demonstrate a range of behaviors that become increasingly detrimental, like cashing in my life savings and moving to the desert. The further we distort or depart from reality, the unhealthier we become.

Is this what happens when people believe in God? Patrick Glynn provides evidence and a stunning answer to that question: [9]

> Ironically enough, scientific research in psychology over the past 25 years has demonstrated that, far from being a neurosis or source of neurosis as Freud and his disciples claim, religious belief is one of the most consistent correlates of overall mental health and happiness.
>
> Study after study have shown a powerful relationship between religious belief and practice on the one hand, and healthy behaviors with regard to such problems as suicide, alcohol and drug abuse, divorce, depression, and perhaps even surprising levels of sexual satisfaction in marriage on the other.
>
> In short, the empirical data run exactly contrary to the supposedly scientific consensus of the psychotherapeutic profession.

David B. Larson, MD, agreed. A psychiatrist trained at Duke who founded and directed the National Institute for Healthcare Research, Dr. Larson observed the same phenomenon and drew this conclusion:

> If a new health treatment were discovered that helped to reduce the rate of teenage suicide, prevent drug and alcohol abuse, improve treatment for depression, reduce recovery time from surgery, lower divorce rates and enhance a sense of well-being, one would

think that every physician in the country would be scrambling to try it.[10]

Larson is saying that *a belief in God* results in all these things, so every physician in the country ought to prescribe it when you come in with a problem. Can you imagine your doctor saying, "Oh, listen, I'm going to operate. Do you believe in God? That will help with your recovery. And your anxiety and depression, too."

I think Freud is right in one sense. If you honestly believe in something that does not exist, you will become less healthy and probably become mentally ill. Yet we have this mountain of evidence indicating that a strong faith in God results in *better* mental health. By Freud's argument, wouldn't that indicate that people who believe in God are not distorting reality because, in fact, God is real?

There it is again. God has placed eternity in the hearts of men.

✻ ✻ ✻

We have now examined three pieces of internal evidence. I started with these because I think they are compelling and difficult to refute. In the next chapter we will look at external evidence. We will enter into the realm of science—a place where the faith of many has been severely challenged. I hope to show that faith and science are not incompatible, and in fact, that science points to the existence of God.

Two

DOES SCIENCE DISPROVE GOD'S EXISTENCE?

According to the Bible, there is clear external evidence for the existence of God. It is all around us, all the time, if we only have eyes to see. Where do we see it? In creation: "God's invisible qualities—his eternal power and divine nature—have been clearly seen, *being understood from what has been made*, so that men are without excuse."[11]

As I will show in this chapter, science is a friend of people who believe in God. Science uncovers the facts about creation, the marvelous ways things work in the natural realm. But to believe in science exclusively—to deny that anything "has been made"—is to close your eyes even to the possibility of a Creator-God. Anyone taking that position immediately faces three huge questions:

1. Where did the universe come from?
2. How did life arise from non-living matter?
3. How did the simple become complex?

Most people who deny God's existence believe evolution provides complete answers for the second and third questions. Indeed, most everyone agrees that evolution on a very small scale is a valid process. Called *micro*evolution, this is the kind of change that can happen *within species*, like Darwin's famous finch beaks. But some use the theory of biological evolution in a much more sweeping way. They claim it provides a framework for understanding how man could evolve from a single cell, which many scientists believe emerged from non-living matter (the "primordial soup"). That's the kind of evolution I'm talking about in this book.

Conflicting Philosophies

The late Stephen Jay Gould was a professor of evolutionary biology at Harvard. He was considered one of the foremost authorities on evolution. Just prior to his death he wrote,

> No scientific theory can pose any threat to religion, for those two great tools of understanding operate in totally separate realms. Science is an inquiry about the factual state of the natural world; religion is a search for spiritual meaning and ethical values.[12]

We saw in the previous chapter how all four questions of existence are inextricably linked. Do you see how Gould's statement attempts to separate the answers to the first two questions from the last two? He is attempting the logically impossible.

Gould was right when he said science is a great tool

for uncovering facts about the state of the natural world. But here's an important caveat: facts do not interpret themselves. Facts need to be blended into systems in order to be understood and given meaning. Those systems are known as *philosophies*. All philosophies prevalent today can be separated into two main categories: *naturalism* and what I call *naturalism-plus*.

Naturalism. Naturalism says the universe is made up exclusively of matter and energy, and the only things that exist are the things you can experience with your senses—what you can see, hear, smell, taste, and/or touch. Science enables us to detect with our senses and analyze with our minds forms of matter and energy we would not otherwise know much about—like atoms, galaxies, and the activity inside a cell. According to naturalists, nothing exists outside of nature; therefore, the supernatural is completely imaginary.

Naturalism-plus. The other category of philosophy can be called supernaturalism, but let's call it naturalism-plus. This is because, in addition to accepting the obvious existence of matter and energy—the reality you can experience with your five senses—naturalism-plus recognizes a reality outside of nature, something supernatural. The vast majority of people on the naturalism-plus side believe that this "something supernatural" is a supremely intelligent and powerful being they call God. Naturalism-plus people who believe in the existence of God are known as *theists*.

It is crucial to understand that the divide is not between science and faith. Faith in the existence of God is not incompatible with science, and science is not incompatible with faith in God. The divide happens between naturalism and naturalism-plus. That is, the divide happens between two different philosophies. Science and faith become *competing* rather than *complimentary* ways of seeing the world only when they get an overlay of naturalist philosophy—a philosophy willing to bend over backwards to interpret scientific facts so that they seem to exclude both the validity of faith and the validity of naturalism-plus.

So don't buy the claim that the conflict is between science and faith. It is not, and it never has been. It has always been between two competing philosophies— naturalism and naturalism-plus. Science is a tool that either side can use well, or use poorly.

The Cake and the Cosmos

Naturalists depend on the theory of evolution to explain how life arose from non-living matter and how the simple became complex. But how do they explain the origin of the universe? For years the naturalist position was this: the universe did not originate—it always was. If such a claim is true, then an infinite amount of time was available for a primordial soup to evolve into complex organisms— a lynchpin presupposition for naturalists.

Picture the universe as an enormous cake. Would there be evidence for the existence of a baker? If the cake has been there for as long as you can remember, and if your genealogy shows the cake was around when your great-great-great-great-grandfather was alive, and if you extrapolate the concept to infinity past—you might conclude that the cake was *always* there. And if the cake always existed, it means no baker was ever on the scene. That is what naturalists believed about the origin of the universe for a long time.

But in 1927, Edwin Hubble, inventor of the powerful telescope named after him, performed an experiment. He passed the light of a distant star through a prism and discovered the light shifted to the red part of the color spectrum. This proved the star was moving further away from earth. It was the same with every star he tested. He called this phenomenon "red shift," and concluded from it that the universe is expanding. This led to what later became known as the Big Bang theory.[13] If the universe is expanding, it must be expanding from someplace, and if you go back far enough it had to expand from a single point, a point that one day must have made a really big bang.

Then, in 1964, two Bell Laboratory scientists, Arno Penzias and Robert Wilson, discovered and began to measure cosmic microwave background radiation. Explained in the simplest terms, if you're out on the Fourth of July watching the fireworks and you see an explosion go off against the darkness, it lights up the sky and then fades. The imprint of the explosion that lingers is a radiation echo. Working backwards in time, Penzias and Wilson used radiation echoes to measure the initial explosion that, they theorize, began the universe.[14] Through a series of related scientific experiments culminating in 1994, scientists proved beyond reasonable scientific doubt that the universe has not always existed.

Carl Sagan, a famous naturalist, began his 1980 TV program, *Cosmos*, the same way every week: "The cosmos is all there is, all there ever was, all there ever will be." Now we know that's all wrong.

Before the Beginning: Ex Nihilo

Genesis 1:1 says, "In the beginning, God created the heavens and the earth." And Hebrews 11:3 says, "By faith we understand that the universe was created by the word of God, so that what is seen was not made out of things that are visible." That is, the Bible tells us that God created the universe out of nothing. Theologians coined a phrase for that concept: *ex nihilo*, "out of nothing." It means that before "God created," not only was there no universe, there was nothing to make a universe *from*—no matter, no energy, and no time. There was also no dimension, meaning there was not even any space for the stuff the universe was made from to *not* exist in. So, there was doubly nothing, if you get my point.

Proponents of the "big bang" explain the creation of the universe through what they call a "singularity." When physicists speak of the expansion of the universe from a singularity they claim that dimension—space itself— expanded with the big bang. There is nothing outside the universe, naturalists claim, so a singularity is a way of saying the universe sprang from a true nothingness.

Theists believe the existence and activity of a Creator is the primary explanation for how something can come from nothing. The beauty and magnificence of the words, "God created" are revealed in this: no mere something came out of nothing, but an entire universe came out of nothing. And not just any universe—a universe containing life. And not just any life—intelligent life, with people like you who can read words and sentences and paragraphs and derive meaning from them.

Theists see the work of Hubble, Penzias, and Wilson as providing credible *scientific* evidence to support the theistic position—creation happened *ex nihilo*! It should have made the front page of *The New York Times*: "Science Finds New Support for the Existence of God." But, go figure, it never has.

Hugh Ross, Ph.D., a highly respected astrophysicist, made this observation:

> As atheistic and agnostic researchers have been repeatedly and progressively pointed by the evidence toward a personal Creator, they have devised more and more bizarre loopholes to escape these findings. This misguided ingenuity will doubtless continue until the return of Christ. However, the evidence for a universe designed, initiated, shaped, and sustained exactly as the Bible describes, by God, continues to mount. [15]

Evidence for Intelligent Design

Intelligent Design is the proposition that the existence of the universe and life are best explained by the activity of an intelligent cause, not random processes such as natural selection. To theists, evidence for intelligent design is evidence for the existence of God.

Let's go back to the cake analogy. Cakes have bakers and bakers have recipes. If you examine a cake carefully, you start to realize there are a bunch of ingredients in it, and they all need to be added in a certain ratio and in a certain sequence and then baked at a certain temperature for a certain amount of time. You have flour, sugar, vanilla, shortening, and eggs. But if you put in a cup of salt instead of a cup of sugar, what should have been a tasty cake comes out an inedible mess. Picture the universe as a cake and ask if there is evidence for a recipe. If there is, chances are there would be a baker to go with it.

Brandon Carter, Ph.D., was a cosmologist and astrophysicist at Cambridge University. In 1973, he went to a conference in Krakow, Poland, and presented a paper to the most prestigious gathering of astrophysicists and astronomers in the world. Called "The Anthropic Principle,"[16] Carter's paper said the universe was made of all kinds of unrelated ingredients, like subatomic particles, strong and weak nuclear forces, electromagnetic radiation, gravity, and three dozen or so other ingredients. He said all of these ingredients had to come together in exact proportions and interact in exact sequences with absolute precision in order for human life on our planet to be sustained. Not merely to make it edible like a cake, but so it would be *livable*. Everything had to be in perfect balance. If even one of these ingredients would go even a tiny fraction of a percent out-of-kilter—POOF—no livable universe!

Carter concluded the universe gives every indication it was designed to the minutest detail with one thing in mind—us. Us! That's why he called it The Anthropic Principle, from the Greek word *anthropos*, meaning man. Not surprisingly, there was an explosion of fury in the scientific community. Carter's paper implied a designer with a recipe, a purposeful God big enough and intelligent enough to manage all the ingredients of an unimaginably immense universe.

The Naturalist Answer: Multiple Universes

The scientific evidence that the universe had a beginning posed a two-fold challenge to naturalist philosophy. First, naturalists had to scramble for a new explanation for the origin of the universe. And, second, they could no longer claim there had been unlimited time for macroevolution to take place.

Naturalists eventually responded with a new category of theories to try to explain how all these precise conditions could come to exist in our universe by chance. The cornerstone idea is that multiple universes must exist simultaneously, each one the result of countless random events. Out of these billions and billions of parallel universes, we happen to be in the one universe where everything came together just right.

It makes me think of billions and billions of cake recipes, where the elements of each recipe are random. Let's simplify that and limit the possible ingredients to actual cake ingredients, but the *proportions* are random. For each recipe there is a bag of ingredients. Some bags have no salt, some have lots of salt, some have no flour, some have lots of flour, some are baked at 1000 degrees, and some are not baked at all. But out of all those billions and billions of bags, eventually one cake popped out that was just right. That, in essence, is the theory of how our hospitable universe could have come about.

But the thing is, that is not science. It involves zero scientific facts. It is philosophy—naturalist philosophy that rejects even the possibility of a "cook" or a "designer" like God.

Alvin Plantinga, a professor of philosophy at Notre Dame, compared this theory to a poker game in the Wild West. The dealer deals himself four aces twenty times in a row. Everybody starts to reach for their guns, and the dealer says, "Wait, wait, wait! I want you guys to think about something. In all the billions and billions of poker games that have gone on in this world and other worlds, don't you think eventually it could happen that a dealer could deal himself four aces twenty times in a row and not be cheating?" And the people around the table would say, "Yeah, that's a possibility. Now we're gonna kill you!"

Because nobody operates on a line of possibility that thin.

Entropy: Another Nuisance for Naturalists

The second law of thermodynamics is also known as the law of entropy. But I prefer to call it The Law of Your Kid's Room. It says that things always proceed from order to disorder unless you infuse the system with intelligence and an outside source of energy. That is why, when you tell your kids, "Go clean your room," they never come back and say, "You know, I left the window open, and the wind was blowing really hard—and the room cleaned itself!" You would not believe them because nothing in our universe ever works that way. At least, apart from the supernatural.

The law of entropy has never been proven wrong. And this law gives naturalists fits when it comes to explaining the origin of life and how something simple can become complex. But for those on the naturalism-plus side, especially the theists, the law of entropy is not troubling at all. Instead, it provides more external evidence for the existence of God—a God with unlimited intelligence and energy to create and sustain life and the entire universe.

The Bible declares that "in [Christ] all things hold together"[17] and that "he upholds the universe by the word of his power."[18] In spite of the obvious fact that everything tends to go from order to disorder, an amazingly intricate network of orderliness is maintained in this world from one moment to the next. How can entropy and a high degree of order coexist in the same universe? Because God holds it together.

Specified Complexity

How did life arise from non-living matter? The naturalist answer goes something like this:

> Chemicals + Time + Random Chance (because nothing directs it) = Life

That's what most of us we were taught in school. Remember the primordial soup? Chemicals are boiling around, on, and under the earth's surface, and then lightning strikes—and all of a sudden life happens.

But in recent years, the tool of science has uncovered several problems with this explanation. The first one came through microbiology, a relatively recent science boosted forward by the invention of the microscope. Better and better microscopes have been developed to the point that today we have scanning electron microscopes that can magnify objects up to two million times, and atomic-force microscopes that can "feel" the electron clouds of atoms. What microbiologists have found is that a single living cell is much more complex than people first thought. In every living cell, thousands upon thousands of *organic machines* run back and forth, taking stuff to and fro.

Michael Denton wrote,

> Magnify a cell a thousand million times until it is twenty kilometers in diameter and resembles a giant airship large enough to cover a great city like London or New York. We would then see an object of unparalleled complexity and adaptive design. On the surface of the cell we would see millions of openings, like the portholes of a vast space ship, opening and closing to allow a continual stream of materials to flow in and out. If we were to enter one of these openings we would find ourselves in a world of supreme technology and bewildering complexity.[19]

William Dembski, Ph.D., is an analytic philosopher and a senior fellow of the Discovery Institute's Center for Science and Culture. In 2002, Dembski introduced a theory called "specified complexity."[20] Simply put, it says the more complicated something is to put together, the more intelligence and energy it takes to actually assemble it. For instance, if you have a lawnmower that is in a thousand pieces, assembling it takes a lot more intelligence and energy than it takes to put together a ham sandwich consisting of only five pieces.

Dembski pointed to the level of complexity in a single living cell and asked the obvious question: How did that come into being without any intelligence? The naturalist's answer is "random processes." But as we will see in the next section, that level of complexity arising out of chaos through random processes is so terribly inefficient that it is essentially a statistical impossibility.

Theists look at the same facts uncovered by the science of microbiology, and they see more external evidence for the existence of a God of inconceivable intelligence, energy, beauty, and majesty.

The Mathematics of Impossibility

The complexity issue becomes even more problematic for naturalists when they face the question of the molecular basis of the origin of life. This issue is brought into focus through the field of applied mathematics.

David Foster studied the probability of a random process producing the DNA for one of the most primitive single cells. He wrote, "The DNA of the T4 bacteriophage has an improbability of 10 to the 78,000th power. In a universe only 10 to the 18th power seconds old, it is obvious that life could not have evolved by random chance."[21]

But what if the universe is older than David Foster says it is? The consensus of today's naturalists claims the universe is 13.7 billion years old. That's less than 10 to the 42nd power seconds old and, according to the mathematics of the Big Bang, still not nearly enough time to explain the complexities of DNA and the origin of life.

Frederick Hoyle was the mathematician who coined the phrase "Big Bang." When he tried to determine how something as complex as a living cell could happen through random processes, he ran the numbers and came up with one chance in 10 to the 40,000th power.[22] To put that number in perspective, you should know that, the total number of atoms in the observable universe is only 10 to the 80th power.[23] By the way, Hoyle was a naturalist, certainly not biased toward the naturalism-plus position, and in his day the scientific understanding of a living cell was incredibly primitive and simplistic—if he were making that estimate today the probability would be *much* smaller.

What it boils down to is this: the probability of life emerging from nonliving matter through a random process is so ridiculously tiny we might even say it is virtually impossible. In fact, with numbers like one chance in 10 to the 40,000th power, the field of applied mathematics may provide the most compelling external evidence for the existence of God.

Genetics, Paleontology and Geology

Over the years, the naturalist explanation for how the simple became complex encountered major challenges from many other disciplines of science. Take the field of genetics. Geneticists discovered you can engineer a lot of changes within a species. You can make really big dogs, and you can make really small dogs, but you cannot make a dog as small as a grasshopper or as big as an elephant. You can make a big dog, but you cannot make a dog with wings. Why not? There are genetic boundaries in place, boundaries so strong there is no way to get around them. Naturalist philosophy cannot explain that scientific fact because their theories predict that the power of randomness should have no limits at all.

Take the fields of paleontology (the study of prehistoric life) and geology (the study of the earth and its fossil record). Darwin said the evolution from simple to complex is a gradual process—so gradual that you cannot see it happen. There may be transitional beings all around you, but you cannot really tell because evolution happens so slowly that you don't notice it. Darwin recognized that the proof for this theory would be in the fossil record:

> Geology assuredly does not reveal any such finely graduated organic chain; and this, perhaps is the most obvious and gravest objection which can be urged against my theory. The explanation lies, as I believe, in the extreme imperfection of the geological record.[24]

In other words, Darwin said, "I realize there is not proof now, but eventually you will find it if you dig long enough. My theory rests on this."

This explains why naturalists are always looking for *the missing link*. Actually, they are not looking for just one link—they need to look for millions of links, because that is what it would take to connect the dots between primordial soup and humans. But after more than 150 years since Darwin's prediction, they still don't have many links. They have just a handful that they say are transitional fossils. In fact, Stephen Jay Gould wrote,

> The extreme rarity of transitional forms in the fossil record persists as the trade secret of paleontology. The evolutionary trees that adorn our textbooks have data only at the tips and nodes of their branches; the rest is inference, however reasonable, not the evidence of fossils.[25]

This prompted Gould to come up with a new theory called "punctuated equilibrium." He says when you dig in the earth you will find that species maintain a state of stasis, staying the same for many, many years; then all of a sudden they transition to a new species, but they do it so fast it does not leave a record.

I just want you to get what he said. This is a professor at Harvard, a foremost authority in evolution during his time, and he said that his theory is based on something happening so fast that it leaves no evidence. That is not science; that is philosophy.

Meanwhile, theists view the lack of a fossil record supporting macroevolution as indirect external evidence for the existence of God.

A Little Advice

When talking to someone who denies the existence of God, avoid discussions about the age of the earth or whether Genesis refers to seven literal 24-hour days or whether there was a worldwide flood. Instead, ask and answer the bigger questions: Is the existence of God compatible with the facts that the tool of science has uncovered? And is it compatible with an honest assessment of what is deep within us?

The Four Questions of Existence from chapter one are a good place to start. Demonstrate how Christianity's answers are consistent with the tool of science *and* coherent through all four questions. It may be helpful to clarify the arena for the conflicts that arise—naturalist versus naturalist-plus philosophy.

Lastly, present your exhibits—the internal and external (scientific) pieces of evidence for the existence of God.

In the process of presenting your evidence, show how Christianity's answers are elegant in their beauty and power, and how they provide a more reasonable and deeply meaningful description of truth than naturalism could ever offer. Display as best you can how the fingerprints of God are seen all over the findings of science, and always have been.

* * *

Let's assume for a moment that God does exist. A lot of what we know about God comes from the Bible. But is the Bible credible? Can we trust it? We will delve into that question in the next chapter

Three
IS THE BIBLE AUTHENTIC AND TRUE?

The Bible is a remarkable book. It was written in three languages, by approximately forty authors, over a period of more than 1600 years. And in spite of all its diversity, the entire Bible has a single theme: God's plan for redeeming fallen mankind.

Perhaps the most remarkable fact about the Bible is that it claims to be inspired by God.[26] In the original languages, the expression "inspired by God" literally means *God-breathed*. In other words, the Bible claims to be the very words of God.

Either that's true, or it isn't.

If the Bible's claim about itself is false, we can safely dismiss it. But if the claim is true, we had better give that book our utmost attention, because there can be no higher authority on earth.

Here is the briefest summary of what's at stake on the question of the whether the Bible contains God's words.

- If the Bible is God-breathed, then all its claims are true.
- If the Bible is God-breathed, we know why there is something rather than nothing.
- If the Bible is God-breathed, we know the broad outlines of the past and the future. We know why this universe exists. We know why we exist. And we know what will remain when there is no longer any trace of the moon, or the earth, or the sun.

But if the Bible is not true, if it is not God-breathed, we know none of these things. This matter of the truth and authenticity of Scripture is one really big deal.

I address two questions in this chapter. The first question asks how we can determine whether the Bible is *authentic*: How do we know that the Bible we have today is what was originally written? The second question relates to whether the Bible is *true*: How do we know the Bible's authors are can be trusted as credible witnesses?

Is Today's Bible Authentic?

Let's face it: the Bible has had a long time to get off track. Even the newest sections of the Bible were written nearly fourteen centuries before the printing press was invented. Many people naturally assume the stories grew out of proportion over time.

You probably know the legend of the lumberjack Paul Bunyan. I suppose he was a big guy in real life. But by the time it was all said and done, people were singing songs about him being "sixty-three axe handles high with his feet on the ground and his head in the sky." That is the way some people think about Jesus, too. They say, "Yeah, Jesus was probably a good man and a great teacher. But then his disciples made him a little bit larger than life, and then people after that made him a little bit bigger, and before you knew it, he was walking on water and giving sight to the blind and doing the whole resurrection thing."

How do we know that the Bible is authentic? That is, how do we know it hasn't expanded over time like the legend of Paul Bunyan? One thing we can do is treat it like any other ancient literature. Historians have designed a method for testing such literature for authenticity. This authenticity test consists of three questions:

1. How early is the earliest copy?
2. How many copies do you have?
3. How much do the copies vary from one to another?

To begin with, there are no original manuscripts of any ancient literature. None. The originals written on parchment or vellum have long since deteriorated. All the documents in existence today are copies. That is why these questions are so important. The closer your earliest copy is to the date of the original writing, the more early copies you have, and the more consistent these copies are to each other, the better off you are.

Questions 1 & 2: The Auditorium of Authenticity

Here is a way to show how the authenticity test works for Questions 1 and 2. I call it the Auditorium of Authenticity.

Imagine an auditorium in which the stage represents the date of the original writing. Each row along the center aisle represents 100 years of time since the original. If you have a copy created 250 years after the original document, for example, it would belong in the aisle halfway between rows two and three. So you collect all the copies of the original document, and place them in the aisles in their proper locations. The closer the documents are to the stage (Question 1) *and* the greater the number of documents you have (Question 2), the more certainty you can have about a document's authenticity.

Let's look at three examples of ancient writings from Aristotle, Julius Caesar, and Homer to see how they stack up to the New Testament in the Auditorium of Authenticity.

Aristotle. Aristotle's logical treatises (known collectively as *The Organon*) were written around 340 BC. According to historians, that was the time of the original writing, the front of the stage. The earliest copy we have is dated AD 1100. That is 1,440 years after the original, and there are five such copies in existence. So in the Auditorium of Authenticity we would place five copies on the center aisle between rows 14 and 15.

Caesar. Julius Caesar wrote *History of the Gallic Wars* in approximately 50 BC. The earliest copy we have is AD 1000. That is 1,050 years after the original. Nine copies exist from that time, so we would place them between the tenth and eleventh row. Julius Caesar's history would have a better authenticity rating than Aristotle's logical treatises because there are more copies, and those copies are closer to the stage.

Homer. Homer wrote *The Iliad* in about 800 BC. The earliest copy is from around AD 250, which is 1,050 years again. Even though Homer wrote centuries before Aristotle and Caesar, 650 manuscripts or partial manuscripts of *The Iliad* have been preserved, so all 650 get placed between rows ten and eleven. The authenticity rating of Homer's *Iliad*, then, would trump Julius Caesar's history by more than seventy times.

The New Testament. The vast majority of historians accept all three of the documents I just mentioned above as authentic. But how does the New Testament compare to them in the Auditorium of Authenticity?

By AD 90, about 60 years after Christ lived on earth, all 27 books of the New Testament had been written. The earliest partial manuscript shows up *before* the front row. It is a little piece of John 18, and it happens to be identical to what is in your translation of the Bible today, except it is written in Greek. At the auditorium's second row we have the entire gospel of Luke, plus the entire gospel of John, plus three more New Testament books in their entirety: 1 Peter, 2 Peter, and Jude. At the third row, we have two complete manuscripts of the entire New Testament.[27] At Row 9, a good century before any of the other ancient documents I mentioned start to appear, we have 5,000 manuscripts. Row 9, 5000![28]

Sir Frederic Kenyon, a paleontologist and president of the British Academy from 1917-1921 wrote, "The interval between the dates of original composition and the earliest manuscripts becomes so small, it is in fact negligible, and the last foundation for any doubt that the

Scriptures have come to us substantially as they were written has been removed."[29]

Question 3: Manuscript Variances

The third question asks, "How much do the copies vary from one another?" If the content of these documents is all over the place, it doesn't mean much to have 5,000 copies close in time to the original. But the greater the consistency between copies, the more confident you can be that the original was accurately passed down through history.

The New Testament is particularly remarkable in this regard. Biblical scholars Norman Geisler and William Nix studied the variances between manuscripts and concluded, "The New Testament, then, has not only survived in more manuscripts than any other book from antiquity [that's Question 2], but it has survived in a purer form [Question 3] than any other great book — a form that is 99.5% pure."[30]

Using the same three-part test we use for other ancient literature, no other document compares to the New Testament in authenticity. That's why we can be confident that the New Testament we have today is a faithful representation of the original writings.

Is the Bible True?

Just because the New Testament is *authentic* does not necessarily mean it is *true*. Historians evaluate the truth of a document by testing it for credibility. Just as there are three basic questions for testing authenticity, there are three more for testing credibility:

1. How credible is the oral testimony of the speakers?
2. How credible is the written testimony of the authors?
3. How credible is the collateral evidence?

For the New Testament, we get *oral testimony* from people who were *quoted* in the various books of the Bible but did not do the actual writing. Jesus is the predominant example.

Written testimony comes from Matthew, Mark, Luke, John, Paul, Peter, James, Jude, and the author of Hebrews.

Questions 1 & 2: Testimony

People who provide testimony — whether oral or written — are called witnesses. And historians agree that by far the best kind of witness to have is an eyewitness.

Eyewitnesses of the Gospel Events. When Luke set out to write his gospel, he started it like this:

> Inasmuch as many have undertaken to compile a narrative of the things that have been accomplished among us, just as *those who from the beginning were eyewitnesses and ministers of the word have delivered them to us*, it seemed good to me also, having followed all things closely for some time past, to write an orderly account for you.[31]

As you can see, Luke made it perfectly clear that everything he would write would come from eyewitness sources.

With the apostle Peter, even this single degree of separation is removed. He didn't merely interview and quote eyewitnesses; he was an eyewitness himself. He wrote in his account, "We did not follow cleverly invented stories when we told you about the power and coming of our Lord Jesus Christ, but *we were eyewitnesses* of his majesty."[32] Peter was there in person.

Of all the eyewitnesses of the life of Jesus Christ, the apostle John was perhaps the most intimate with him. John was emphatic about his witness being first-hand when he wrote this:

> That which was from the beginning, which we have heard, which we have seen with our eyes, which we looked upon and have touched with our hands, concerning the word of life—the life was made manifest, and we have seen it, and testify to it and proclaim to you the eternal life, which was with the Father and was made manifest to us—that which we have seen and heard we proclaim also to you.[33]

In many cases second-, third- and even fourth-hand testimony are accepted today as historical fact. But here in the case of the New Testament, we have multiple-source, highly personal, eyewitness accounts (both oral and written testimony) provided in the documents themselves. It all leads to an impressively high level of credibility. And the evidence just gets better from here.

Contemporaneous Witnesses. Whenever and wherever the apostles preached, they addressed people who were alive at the time and place that Jesus lived and taught and performed miracles. For example, in his first sermon, Peter says, "Men of Israel, hear these words: Jesus of Nazareth, a man attested to you by God with mighty works and wonders and signs that God did through him *in your midst, as you yourselves know.*"[34] Later, Paul is giving a response to a king and essentially says, "I know that you know this stuff because it wasn't done in a corner."[35]

This matter of having contemporaneous witnesses is really important. Consider that John F. Kennedy was assassinated in 1963. Now, suppose I was so enamored with Kennedy that I considered myself his disciple and wanted to start a cult about him in my town. And suppose I knew I would have to exaggerate and lie to get it going, but I used the handy excuse that the ends justify the means. I would start preaching, "President Kennedy was a great man, but he was much more than that. When he made his campaign stop here in Hudson, he got out of his car, healed a bunch of blind and sick people and then went to the Redmond Funeral Home and raised a couple people from the dead!" Somebody would say, "Wait a minute! I was there that day and none of that ever happened!" I would ignore the outburst and say, "Hey, the next afternoon Jack took a Happy Meal and fed the whole town with it." And someone else would say, "You nutcase! I was in Hudson the next day and he did nothing of the sort!" That's probably about the time I would give up on my plan to start a Kennedy Cult.

Since the apostles told their stories about Jesus to

people who were alive at the time and place where Jesus lived, the credibility of their testimony goes through the roof. Because if their stories were made up, they could never have gotten away with it.

Question 3: Collateral Evidence

Another way to evaluate the credibility of a witness is to determine whether "the rest of the story" checks out. This is known as collateral evidence.

Suppose I witness a crime in a theatre parking lot. On the witness stand, I'd be asked, "Mr. Coffey, tell us what happened on the evening of April 23." I would say, "Well, I was coming out of the theater. I'd gone to see the 9:30 showing of *Finding Nemo*, and I had my Whoppers, because I always buy Whoppers when I go to a movie. I walked out and then I saw this thing happen." A good defense attorney would investigate to see if all of the parts of my story checked out. What if he discovered there was no 9:30 showing of *Finding Nemo* on April 23? And what if the theatre did not sell Whoppers? The collateral evidence would not be corroborated and I would be discredited as a witness.

For years, critics of the Bible tried to find contradictions in the collateral evidence of Scripture. They focused on Luke in particular, because Luke wrote as an historian. In the Gospel of Luke and the Book of Acts he names all kinds of people and places that can be checked out. Historians seized on these statements and for a while thought they could prove either that Luke was lying or that Luke the Apostle was not the author of Luke and Acts at all.

For example, Luke 3:1-2 says the word of God came to John the Baptist when Lysanias was the tetrarch of Abilene. For years critics said, "Aha! We know that Lysanias died 30 years before John the Baptist was born—we know that for a fact. So Luke was lying about that, and that discredits him as a witness." However, an inscription dated between AD 14-29 was eventually discovered that said "Lysanias, tetrarch of Abilene"—the exact time Luke said Lysanias was tetrarch of Abilene. And the critics said, "Oh, there must have been two Lysaniases. Sorry about that."[36]

Luke's writings refer to a total of 32 countries, 54 cities, and 9 islands. One archeologist found that these references have turned out to be 100 percent accurate.[37] Today, critics can no longer support their claim that Luke didn't write the gospel of Luke and the Book of Acts. The collateral evidence of authenticity in Luke's writing is just too strong.

Eyewitnesses Revisited: Ulterior Motives

Let's go back to my example about President Kennedy. Imagine that despite the fact that all kinds of people could testify that what I was saying about Kennedy's visit to Hudson was bunk, I held tight to my story. I kept on preaching about the Kennedy Miracles (to which I claimed to be an eyewitness) because I *really* wanted people to join me. We've already seen how unlikely it is that anyone would pay attention, but stay with me here—because we can't ignore the fact that sometimes people lie.

If a witness has something to gain by saying one thing

instead of another, the credibility of that witness becomes suspect. Like during a big criminal trial when the prosecutors make a plea bargain with a key witness: the witness is probably a criminal who had his sentence reduced or dropped in exchange for his testimony against the guy on trial. Isn't it obvious that an offer like that has great potential for causing a witness to lie, or at least to deliberately have a selective memory?

That can certainly happen. So, what about the witnesses to the events of the life of Jesus? Were they like me in the Kennedy example, peddling fables for fame? I recently heard someone say, "Yeah, the disciples made up the stories so they could get rich and famous." He could not have been more wrong.

Jesus had twelve disciples. Judas hanged himself after he betrayed Jesus; that left eleven. History records that out of the eleven original disciples, ten died violent deaths they could have avoided had they simply said, "Okay, it's not true. Jesus did not rise from the dead. We made it all up."

I always thought that if ten people were all clinging to the same lie, and you put me in a room with them and gave me absolute power, I could find out the truth. I would probably only have to kill one guy. I would walk in and yell, "Listen, I'm looking for the truth." Boom! I'd shoot Pat, and Pat drops over. Then I'd point the gun at the next person and say, "Tell me the truth!" Do you think *you'd* still stick with the lie at that point? But if the next person did, I'd shoot him. And just go down the line until I found someone who decided the lie was not worth dying for.

That is essentially what happened to all ten disciples.

But in 2,000 years, not a single shred of evidence has been uncovered to show that any of them even wavered. Each one went to his death saying, "It's true, it's true."

To die for a lie is rare. For ten eyewitnesses to die for the same lie is against all odds.

Simon Greenleaf, one of the founders of Harvard Law School, set out to disprove Christianity. He performed an extensive study of the credibility of the gospel witnesses and the evidence for and against the resurrection, all from a legal standpoint. He ended up concluding: "Let the Gospels' testimony be sifted, as it were given in a court of justice on the side of the adverse party, the witness being subjected to a rigorous cross examination. The result, it is confidently believed, will be undoubting conviction of their integrity, ability, and truth."[38]

Truth, Not Legend

So we have the Auditorium of Authenticity test. We have the test of manuscript variances. We can scrutinize the oral and written testimony as well as the collateral evidence found in the New Testament books. We can also evaluate the likelihood of whether those witnesses behind those original documents were lying. And when you put it all together, the evidence is overwhelming. The New Testament books, featuring a central character known as Jesus of Nazareth, check out as being far more authentic and far more credible than any other ancient documents.

And that's how we know there is no "Paul Bunyan effect" when it comes to stories in the Bible about Jesus' life.

What about the Old Testament?

We could go through the same steps for the Old Testament and come up with the same conclusions. But I will save that for another book. For now, consider this argument. *If* we can safely assume the New Testament is the Word of God, then the Old Testament also qualifies. Why? Because the New Testament speakers and writers, with one accord, testify that the Old Testament is God's Word.

When Jesus said, "Man shall not live by bread alone, but by every word that comes from the mouth of God,"[39] he was not merely quoting the Old Testament.[40] He was indicating it is the Word of God. And while chiding the Pharisees for elevating the significance of their traditions, Jesus directly called the Old Testament "the word of God."[41] And if time and space allowed, I could show you where all the other New Testament speakers and writers unanimously concur.

So we have the New Testament testifying about the Old Testament. And in turn—one factor that makes the Bible hold together so well as a single book—the Old Testament predicts events recorded in the New Testament!

The Witness of Prophecy

If the Bible is the Word of God, we would expect its every prediction about the future to come true with precise accuracy. Did you know that the Bible contains the *only* sacred texts of the major religions that make detailed prophecies?[42] Our Bible has hundreds of prophecies. In venturing to make these predictions, the Bible puts its credibility at risk, because if any single one of them failed, it would prove the Bible was not the Word of God.

The prophesies of the Bible cover dozens of different topics. But for our purposes I will zero in on the Old Testament prophecies related to the coming of the Messiah, namely Jesus of the New Testament. There are at least 60 Old Testament prophecies quoted in the New Testament as fulfilled by Jesus.[43] Describing those prophesies and their fulfillment is enough to fill up a whole book, so I will mention just sixteen of the best-known. For starters, here are six written at least 450 years before Jesus was born:

- His mother would be a virgin.[44]
- He would be of the seed of Abraham.[45]
- He would be descended from Isaac.[46]
- He would be of the tribe of Judah.[47]
- He would be of the house of David.[48]
- His birthplace would be Bethlehem, a tiny village.[49]

Can you imagine trying to predict where your great-great-great-great-great-great-great-great-grandson would be born—not just the state or even the country, but the very town? Newborn babes cannot control their ancestry or their place of birth. Yet the birth of Jesus fulfilled all six of these highly specific prophesies.

The Old Testament also predicted the Messiah would perform miracles[50] and cleanse the temple.[51] It predicted he would be rejected and mocked by his own people[52] and be silent before his accusers.[53] It predicted his hands and feet would be pierced [54] and people would cast lots for his clothing, [55] that he would be crucified with thieves [56] and would pray for his persecutors. [57] It predicted his side would be pierced [58] and that he would be buried in a rich man's tomb. [59] That's sixteen prophecies, each one perfectly fulfilled.

Peter Stoner is a mathematician who studied the odds of prophecies coming true. He calculated the odds of just eight prophecies coming true by random chance in any one person's lifetime. It is one in a hundred million billion. [60] That is a big number to wrap your head around, so he used an illustration to help put it into perspective. It basically goes like this.

Take the state of Texas (we're talking 268,820 square miles) and fill it with silver dollars two feet deep. Then take one silver dollar, mark it with a red "x," shoot it with a big cannon into the middle of the state, and stir it all up with a big Texas-sized spoon. Next, pick a guy out of a crowd, blindfold him, spin him around, and tell him to walk to where he thinks that particular silver dollar is. (Give him some snowshoes so he can walk on top of the silver dollars.) Tell him to then dig down as deep into those silver dollars as he wants to, pick just one of them, and try to make it the one with the red x. What are the chances? One in a hundred million billion.

Again, that's the chances of only eight prophecies being fulfilled, not the sixteen we just looked at. But the fact is that Jesus fulfilled *at least* 60 biblical prophecies. What does that tell you about the odds of the Bible truly being the Word of God?

Personal Witness: Intrinsic Evidence

Here is the final reason I believe the Bible is true. It is the evidence I find inside myself. Let me explain. The Bible showed me how I could have peace with God. It told me, "Joe, if you confess with your mouth that Jesus is Lord and believe in your heart that God raised him from the dead, you will be saved."[61] In 1979, I decided to try that, and it worked, and I have never been the same. Everything I have ever tested in the Bible since that time has eventually proven true, starting with the transformation of my own life.

Over the years I have watched firsthand as the Bible has transformed hundreds, even thousands of people, exactly the way it promises to—if we truly put our faith in Jesus Christ and follow the Bible as God's Word.

* * *

So far we have covered some compelling evidence for believing in the existence of God and accepting the Bible as the Word of God. And yet, many who once believed have rejected the faith when they have encountered pain and suffering and the presence of evil in the world. They wonder, "How can God exist, if he allowed this to happen? How can the Bible be true, when it promises abundant life, but this happened to me?" In the next chapter, we will address these kinds of obstacles to faith.

Four

THE QUESTION OF EVIL AND SUFFERING

The existence of evil and suffering present a classic stumbling block to Christian faith—sometimes nearly as much so for Christians as for non-Christians. The universal reality of evil and suffering raises two kinds of questions: philosophical/intellectual ones (questions of the mind), and emotional ones (questions of the heart). You will hardly ever find somebody who has a purely intellectual problem with Christianity. The crises produced by evil and suffering are almost always about both the head and the heart.

The psalmist wrote, "One thing God has spoken, two things have I heard: that you, O God, are strong, and that you, O Lord, are loving."[62] Those two things about God are easy to swallow—until something really bad happens. Then, when doubt and anger set in, we demand some answers.

This is a book on apologetics. Its goal is to equip you

to speak more effectively about Christianity to unbelievers. But since everyone suffers, maybe the best way to equip you is to help you understand. When your own questions about evil and suffering are better settled in your soul, you will be better able to talk about these things to others.

Can Suffering and God Coexist?

When we witness suffering, or when we suffer ourselves, the tendency for both the believer and unbeliever is for the heart and the head to focus on the same question: *Why? Why do such awful, horrible things happen?* From there, the natural human inclination is to think along these lines:

- If the God of the Bible is *loving*, why does he *allow* evil and suffering?
- If the God of the Bible is *powerful*, why doesn't he *stop* evil and suffering?
- Yet evil and suffering are everywhere, so it seems as though:
  > either the God of the Bible does not exist,
  > or the God of the Bible is loving but not powerful,
  > or the God of the Bible is powerful but not loving.

My little brother, John, was killed in a motorcycle accident. He hit a truck head-on. He was twenty years old. It made absolutely no sense to me. I was saying, "God, I love my brother and if *I* could have stopped this from happening, I would have. But now he's dead. So I want to know—did you just not have the 'want to'? But, even if you wanted to, is it just that you couldn't? Is that why my little brother is dead?"

My head was spinning—but my heart was screaming. Both my head and my heart demanded an answer to the same question: Why?

A Man Who Really Suffered

There is an entire book of the Bible dedicated to answering the question of evil and suffering. It is the book of Job. God described Job as "a blameless and upright man, who fears God and turns away from evil."[63] Yet a series of catastrophes rob Job of all his possessions— everything! And then he loses all his children! Next he is afflicted from "head to toe" with an agonizing disease.

Job's wife offers some advice: "Curse God and die."[64] Nice. But Job refuses and literally ends up on an ash heap. All of this, we are told, is at the hand of Satan. Meanwhile, God is fully aware and allows all of it. Throughout the first 37 chapters, Job asks the "why" question in a dozen different ways. But through the entire book of Job, God never gives him an answer.

Job had some friends who, in their zeal to defend God, tried to give Job some answers. At the end of the book, God is really mad at Job's friends. In essence, God says to Job, "You better pray for your friends! They have really ticked me off by trying to give you reasons for all this. But in the process, all they did was trivialize your pain."[65]

Be very careful when you talk to somebody who is really suffering. People who are experiencing deep pain and loss are often angry with God. Do not be like Job's friends. Do not try to defend God by attempting to answer the "why" question. That approach will probably backfire. Remember, it's the heart that hurts, and when the pain is bad, reason can only speak to the mind—it can't even reach the heart. So be really careful what you say.

The Traditional Theories on Suffering

Theologians have come up with three theories on how it can be possible for God to be both loving and powerful, and still bad things happen. Each theory offers some reasonable answers for the head, although none of them is perfect.

The Punishment Theory

God created the world without pain and suffering, but Adam rebelled against God and as a result the whole human race came under God's curse. There is pain and suffering in the world because we are being punished for rebelling against God. At the individual level, punishment is compounded as the result of our own personal brand of rebellion. In essence, that is the punishment theory.

The problem with this theory is the distribution of suffering. All of us are rebels, right? But some of us have gone through a lot more suffering than others. And that doesn't seem fair. Especially when a relatively good person suffers or a relatively bad person gets by scot-free. In cases like those, the punishment theory fails to provide satisfying answers.

The Free Will Theory

This theory says that in order for love to exist, you must have freedom. Unless I am free to choose actions of hatred and evil, my choices to love and do good mean nothing—I would be a robot, and robots cannot love. So, evil and pain and suffering must be allowed to exist in order for love and goodness to be genuine. This is how a God who is both loving and powerful can permit wickedness in the world he has made.

Here is an example of how free will and the potential for pain are connected.

I taught each of my three kids how to ride a two-wheeler the same way. I removed the training wheels and had the child put on a thick sweatshirt. We went out into the street and the child got on the bike. I grabbed the back of the sweatshirt and said, "Start peddling!"

I'd hold on, running alongside, righting the child at each slip. As long as I was holding on, my children did not experience any pain and had a blast.

But every one of my kids at some point turned to me and said the same thing: "Let go! Let go!" It is the cry of the human heart. Freedom. "Let me do it!" So I did. And as I let go of the sweatshirt I knew sooner or later that child would experience pain. Was that my fault? Yes and no. My children needed and wanted freedom, but with freedom comes a real potential for pain.

Here is the problem with the free will theory. If God is both loving and powerful, free will should be important, but it should not be the *most* important thing.

For example, if I saw my young son pedaling into

traffic, I would not sit back and think, "This is really going to end poorly, but I don't want to violate his free will." No! I would run and knock him off his bike, and when he realized what could have happened, he would thank me for violating his free will. But I could not tell God that when my little brother died. I said, "God, why didn't you violate John's free will and let him live?"

There is another problem with the free will theory: distribution. Just like with the punishment theory, it doesn't explain why some people go through a lot more suffering than others.

The Natural Law Theory

The third theory says that laws have been set in place to govern everything in the universe. These laws are necessary for the universe to run properly. According to this natural law theory, certain kinds of actions always have the same consequences. So if you know the laws, you can predict the repercussions of breaking them.

When I was a kid I got hurt all the time. The vast majority of my pain was caused by natural law. I fell out of trees. I ran into hard objects. I've had more than 60 stitches just from my neck up, and no more than five at a time. Mass plus velocity equals impact. The laws of physics bend for no man . . . or boy.

Moral laws are also woven into the fabric of the universe. A teenage girl came into my office once. She had been sexually active and became pregnant. She looked at me with red-rimmed eyes and asked in all sincerity, "How could God do this to me?" She had violated a moral law and this was a predictable consequence.

We make wrong choices and get hurt when we violate natural law. But *not all* of our suffering is a result of our choices. Last month I performed the funeral for a friend who died of lung cancer, though she had never smoked a cigarette in her life. We all know stories like that. The natural law theory fails to provide adequate explanations for all kinds of suffering.

Suffering: Answers for the Head

If the punishment, free will, and natural law theories cannot provide a comprehensive, rational explanation for the existence of evil and suffering, what can?

Let me summarize the logic that underlies the thinking of much (probably most) head-related unbelief: "I do not see a single good reason for this, and because I cannot see one, a reason does not exist." This kind of arrogance can blind us from seeing the truth. Let me use an illustration to explain what I mean.

When my son was two, he fell and cut his eyelid and had to have stitches (he got off to a strong start, and I was a little concerned at first, but he's all grown up now, and I totally have him beat in the stitches department). I took him to the emergency room, and they put him in something the nurse called a "papoose." But it was really a straightjacket that strapped in his arms and his legs so he couldn't move. I held his head because he did not understand. I was trying to calm him. I kept saying, "Jeremy, it's going to be okay. Son, it's okay, it's okay." But when the needle from the doctor first went into the open wound and it stung, Jeremy looked up at me, and his eyes accused me of the worst kind of betrayal. He screamed at the top of his lungs, "It *not* okay!" He could not conceive of a good reason why I would allow him to be subjected to the excruciating pain he experienced at that moment.

Consider Scope and Scale

My first answer for the head is simply this. If there is a God big enough for you to be mad at for allowing whatever evil or pain and suffering has happened, then that God is big enough to have reasons you and I cannot begin to understand.

Let's go back to when my little brother was killed and I demanded an answer to the "why" question. What if God had come down and said to me, "Joe, you wanted to know the answer, so I decided to jot it down. Here you go. But I need to warn you, it's a little complicated. I use a lot of advanced math. There are several dimensions that you don't know exist, and there are people that I will mention who haven't even been born yet. But you demanded I answer the 'why' question, so here you go."

What would I do? I would take it, look it over, and eventually throw my hands up and say, "My brother is still gone, I still have pain, and God answering the 'why' question does not do *anything* for me." Maybe that's why God never answered it for Job. Or me. Or you.

Speaking through the prophet Isaiah, God put it like this: "For my thoughts are not your thoughts, neither are your ways my ways. . . . For as the heavens are higher than the earth, so are my ways higher than your ways and my thoughts than your thoughts."[66] These words are intended to remove our arrogance and give us big, loving arms where we can confidently rest our minds.

Consider Our Response to Evil

What about the people who do not believe in God because of all the pain and suffering in the world? They see new reports of violence and injustice and they shake their heads and say, "See? That is absolutely appalling! There can only be one answer: there is no God." But that answer does not solve the question of evil and suffering. Let me explain.

If God did not create human beings, evolutionary theory tells us that we came about through a process of natural selection—meaning that particular creatures that are better adapted to their environments are more likely to survive and reproduce. In that world, there is no "good" and there is no "evil." The only important thing is whether, or how much, you manage to reproduce before you die.

This means that if God did not create us, we cannot logically talk in terms of good versus evil. Why? For the same basic reason that, unless light exists, it makes no sense to talk about darkness. We cannot define evil apart from a good that stands in contrast to it. And that means there must be some external, objective reality by which good and evil can be measured. The Bible identifies this external, objective reality as God. The Bible says that God is holy, that God is love, that God is merciful and patient and kind. Everything that is unlike God and opposed to him is evil.

So when a woman systematically drowns her four

children, one after another, we are horrified. Mothers aren't supposed to do this. We all know this act is deeply evil. However confused or mentally unstable the woman may have been, what she did was wicked. We react in a similar way to the atrocities of racism, slavery, oppression, classism, genocide, and child trafficking. We know they are evil.

But how do we know? Why have people in every culture throughout history known that some things are good and some things are evil? If we simply evolved by natural selection, those categories make little or no sense. But if we were created by a God who is himself holy and good, they make perfect sense.

The person who sees evil in the world and concludes there is no God has got it backwards. The existence of evil does not tell us there is no God. Instead, our ability to recognize evil tells us there *is* a God.

So when someone says he has seen such appalling evil that he must conclude God doesn't exist, he still has not dealt with the underlying problem—the existence of evil. The intellectually consistent answer is to admit, no matter how ironic it may sound, that because evil exists, God must exist as well.

Suffering: Answers for the Heart

Let's move from the head to the heart. If you are in pain and you have gone through suffering, what *does* help? When my little brother died, I remember asking God the question, "Why?" over and over again. If you have gone through any kind of pain, you cannot get away from the "why" question. You become obsessed with it. But asking that question rarely helps you feel better.

What *did* help when my little brother died was when somebody who had gone through suffering would come and sit with me. I was involved with the church, so lots of people came, but I did not trust anyone who hadn't gone through real pain. I had a particular affinity toward people who had also lost brothers. I still do.

The people that meant the most were the ones that just sat and wept with me. If you've gone through pain, you understand what I mean. They would weep with me and say, "I will sit by your side, and I will walk through this with you." That is the only thing that helped.

The God Who is With Us in Our Pain

Did you know that Christianity is the only religion in the world that has a God who suffers? No other religion even remotely suggests that the God of the universe has ever put himself into the position of suffering. But in Christianity, evil and suffering is such a huge problem for us that it was a problem for God, too. God dealt with the problem by personally entering into evil and suffering. That is why the Son of God came into the world.

Eighteen months after my little brother died, when I was still mad at God, a Bible verse broke through to me. It is the shortest verse in the Bible, which says, "Jesus wept."[67] All of a sudden, the deep meaning of those two words and their application to my life became clear. The God of the universe sits beside me and feels my pain. And he weeps.

God will rarely, if ever, answer the "why" question

for you. Instead, he draws you close and whispers, "I will weep with you, and not only will I weep with you, I know what it feels like to experience unimaginable evil and excruciating pain of every kind." When God sent his Son into the world, Jesus didn't wave a magic wand to make evil and suffering go away. Instead, he entered into the pain and suffering and evil of our world and then, out of unimaginable love, he went to the cross to deal with the evil in you and me.

The God Who Redeems our Suffering

Jesus is "the founder and perfecter of our faith, who for the joy that was set before him endured the cross."[68] One translation of this verse uses "pioneer" instead of "founder." I like to think of Jesus as the pioneer who blazed the trail from evil to joy. He offers to enter into our pain and walk beside us on the trail he blazed. He wipes our tears, points the way forward, and whispers, "Somewhere along this trail you will find your suffering has been redeemed, and you will experience the presence of the love of God that will make a lifetime of suffering seem like a single night spent in a bad hotel."

My second missionary trip was very, very difficult. I was twenty-five years old, and I was leading the trip with my older brother, Brian. At one point, our team had gone too long without food and water. We were sick with dysentery and exhausted and freezing, traveling through the coldest part of the southern Bolivian mountains on an all-night train ride. We were going from a town called Uyuni to another called Wanuni, and I thought, "How much different can it be?" We had been staying in flop-houses the entire trip. We hadn't even *seen* a hotel. The flophouses had a single bathroom on each floor and rarely had running water. Those that did have running water didn't have *hot* water. There was no heat in these places, and there was no good food. It was awful. Those towns were terrible in every way, and here we were travelling all night from Uyuni to Wanuni.

I remember that train ride like it was yesterday. I had pulled all the clothes out of my bag and put them on, and I was still shivering. In the twilight mode between wake-fulness and sleep, I heard a person start to whimper and listened for a while before realizing that the person crying was me! It was pitiful. I sat there in total misery.

When we got to Wanuni, my brother and I sent the team ahead of us before getting in the last taxi and heading down the road. As we rounded the final corner, there it was: five stories high, and lit up in big block letters was "Hotel Terminal."

Brian and I walked in and it smelled like . . . a hotel! Then we went to our rooms and discovered each had its own bathroom! I opened the shower curtain, and there were two knobs . . . *two knobs!* I turned on the hot water knob, and actual hot water gushed out.

Everyone took hot showers, put on clean clothes, and went to the hotel restaurant. We all ordered steak and eggs. We sat around the table and laughed until the tears rolled down our cheeks! But why were we laughing?

We were *not* laughing because it was such a great hotel. You don't walk into the Four Seasons and start laughing uproariously, do you? We weren't laughing because someone made up new jokes. *We were laughing because the pain of the night before was being redeemed.*

We were laughing and stuffing our faces with steak and eggs, and someone would turn to me and say, "Coffey? Was that you crying last night on the train?" And I'd say, "I was miserable! Man, I was freezing!" We had all been cold. And we had all been hungry. But we weren't cold and hungry anymore.

Our tears of pain had turned into tears of joy —*our tears had been redeemed.*

Christianity is the only religion in the world that has a God who will suffer *for you* and then enter into the midst of your pain and sit *beside you*. And weep.

He is the only God who has blazed the trail from the cross to joy so that your tears here on earth will become tears of joy in heaven someday. One day I will sit with my little brother, John, and we will laugh until the tears roll down our faces. But we will not be laughing at how wonderful heaven is. We will be laughing because our tears here have finally been redeemed.

The God of Christianity is unique. And no mistake about it—Christianity properly understood and applied is the only religion that offers deep, satisfying answers to the problem of evil and suffering for both the head *and* the heart.

* * *

It is true that there are many religions in the world. Don't all of them have merit? Are they all essentially the same? We will address these questions next.

Five

AREN'T ALL RELIGIONS THE SAME?

Jesus said, "I am the way and the truth and the life. No one comes to the Father except through me."[69] Can the exclusivity of Jesus' claim be any clearer? He claimed to be *the* way, *the* truth, *the* life. He claimed to be *the only* path to God the Father.

It's because of these claims that the critics shake their heads and say, "That's what I hate about Christianity! You people think you are right and everybody else is wrong!" Such critics have been influenced by a belief that flows through the cultural bloodstream. This belief acts like an antibody—it renders people nearly immune to acknowledging *even the possibility* that one religion could be true and another one false. The theological term for this belief is religious pluralism.

When you start to talk about Jesus to people who have been inoculated by religious pluralism, they might reply, "Oh, listen, I believe all religions are basically the same." This is supposed to be a conversation stopper, a definitive end to any talk about Jesus being who he claimed to be. Religious pluralists are often polite, but inside some may be screaming, "Take your insulting, exclusivist message somewhere else and don't waste any more of my time!" And if religious pluralism is true, then these people are right—the claims of Bible-believing Christians are indeed arrogant and insulting and cruel.

It's not like you can entirely blame religious pluralists for their fears. Exclusivity has done some terrible things in the world. Exclusivity can easily result in a group of people feeling superior and looking down their noses at others. That kind of attitude is culturally repulsive *and* dangerous. Think Adolph Hitler and the Third Reich. Racism is another classic example. Racism has done unspeakable damage around the world and to our nation. Untold numbers of families and individuals have been irreversibly scarred by it.

What an irony—people can reject the beauty and wonder of the gospel simply because they can't accept even the possibility that something good could also be exclusive.

Paul's Take on Religious Pluralism

So how did religious pluralism, this rejection of exclusivity, become so common? In North America, as well as in many other parts of the world, you need look no further than your own neighborhood to find one of the prime reasons—the rise of immigration and the resulting cultural diversity. This trend has produced very interesting social dynamics, and in several ways has made talking about Jesus more challenging.

Suppose a Hindu family moves in next door. At first you may not know what to expect. But you quickly find out they are wonderful people and fantastic neighbors. You think, "Am I really ready to tell them Hinduism is wrong and Christianity is right?" When your kids go off to college they meet all kinds of people. They might come home and say, "I now have friends who come from all over the world, and you need to know that some of my non-Christian friends are better people than some of my Christian friends."

None of this is really new, however. The gospel has been rubbing up against religious pluralism for 2000 years. In Acts 17, Luke reported on the apostle Paul's visit to Athens, which back then was the religious diversity capital of the world. Athens was home to Epicureans, Stoics, Pagans, Jews, and Greeks—all kinds of people with all kinds of beliefs. And it was a city full of religious idols. Anything and everything was acceptable when it came to religion. The multicultural Athenians saw their unbridled religious tolerance as a virtue.

But Paul did not take a walk through the streets of Athens and conclude, "Well, I guess they're all set with their beliefs here, and some of them seem like pretty good people, so I'll just move on." Nor did he say, "Boy, this is a tough crowd. If I start telling them that Jesus is the only way to God, things might get uncomfortable." Instead, he was greatly distressed because the people did not know the truth about salvation through Jesus Christ. So he approached them with respect—and then he brought them the exclusive truth about the exclusive Good News.

To some degree, exclusivity will always separate. It forces a situation where some people are "in" and the rest are "out." That's one of the biggest reasons why a conversation about Christianity versus other religions can become uncomfortable—it turns into us-versus-them, superior-versus-inferior, in-versus-out. If you have been in "discussions" with family members, friends, or neighbors on this topic, you know the scene can quickly become emotionally charged.

- You may talk about Jesus with one person who says, "I believe all religions teach people to be good; every religion has a slightly different way of doing it. Christianity offers a process to make people good. But so does Buddhism. So does Hinduism. There are a lot of ways up the mountain."

- You might talk about Jesus with someone else who says, "Wait! Are you telling me only Christians are going to heaven? And all the other people in the world are going to hell? I don't believe in Jesus, so I'm going to go to hell? Is that what you're saying?" You may think, "Wow, *is* that what I'm saying?"

- You might hear others say, "You know what? You shouldn't push your beliefs on people. The thing I don't like about you born-again Christians is you are always trying to convert people. Just keep it to yourself."

These are undoubtedly tough situations. Exclusivity has never played well in a diverse society, whether 21st-century North America or first-century Athens. Paul spent a lot of time either recovering from beatings or sitting in jail because he refused to stop preaching exclusivity. Like nearly all the apostles, he was eventually executed because he preached exclusivity.

Jesus was very clear that the gospel will never be a universally welcome message.[70] Yet it is a message we must share. Because if what Jesus said about himself in the Bible is true, then his is the most important message mankind could ever hear.

So, what do we do?

In chapter four I said it's rare for someone to have a purely intellectual problem with Christianity. It is nearly always head *and* heart. This is also true when addressing the issues of pluralism and exclusivity. The solution involves the head first, and then the heart.

Exclusivity: Answers for the Head

The basic position of religious pluralism is that all religions lead to God. But if you can be gracious and kind and respectful, you can help religious pluralists begin to see a fundamental problem with this claim. I call it the House on Fire.

Many Ways to Heaven: The House on Fire

The Bible says God made *one* way by sending his Son to die an excruciating death on the cross. The level of Jesus' pain was beyond imagination on every level—physically, emotionally, and spiritually. He did it to make a way— one way—so that sinners could be saved, find their way back to God, and enjoy him in heaven forever and ever. With that in mind, here's an illustration to show why it makes no sense for God to do that *if* there are many ways to be saved.

Suppose my house is on fire and it is full of people I care about. My son, Jeremy, is a big guy. Suppose Jeremy runs up to me screaming, "Dad! The house is on fire! I'm going to throw myself against the burning door and break through it to give people a way to get out!" I would say, "If you do that, you're going to fall right into the flames!" But he says, "Yeah, I know, but it's the only way." I could picture myself maybe saying, "Go!" And the son I love, my only son, would run and break through the burning door and die an excruciating death, but then all the people who were in the house would be saved. That sacrifice makes some sense.

But suppose somebody says, "There are dozens of ways out of the house, and some of them are really easy ways. All you have to do is walk and you're out of the house." Let's say there are 48 different ways out of the house. In that case there is no way any father would send his only son to die an excruciating death to make the 49th way. That makes *no* sense! And it makes no sense to say that you believe Christianity is just one of many ways.

All Claims are Truth Claims: The Pluralist Paradox

Here is another important point that can help religious pluralists if you approach them the right way. They need to see that all truth claims are one person's (or one like-minded group's) description of what is real—of what reality is like.

This point hinges on the key statement that *every truth claim is exclusive by nature*. In other words, whenever two truth-claims conflict, one is right and the other is wrong. Both of them cannot be true at the same time. Conflicting truth claims are mutually exclusive.

If you say the world is round, and I say the world is flat, we have both made exclusive truth claims—both cannot be true at the same time. One claim must be right and the other wrong. Suppose I go up to a husband and wife, and I look at the wife and ask, "Are you pregnant?" (I would never recommend doing this.) She says, "Yes," but at the exact same moment her husband says, "No." Their truth claims are their descriptions of reality, and they both can't be true at the same time.

This same principle applies to religious pluralism when someone says there is only one way and somebody else says there are many ways. *Both* of those are truth claims. *Both* of those claims are *exclusive*. And only one of them is true; the other must be false.

The pluralist who says, "Christianity bugs me because they think their way is the only way," doesn't realize that once he makes that statement, he has also entered an exclusive arena: if he is right, everyone who thinks there is only one way must be wrong. The opponents of exclusivity fall victim to their own argument. I call this the Pluralist Paradox.

All Claims are Truth Claims: "No One Can Know"

If you meet a really good, experienced pluralist, he or she will say something like, "No one can know if their way is the right way. You can't know, and I can't know. Nobody can know for sure." But in Christianity, we believe God revealed himself, and it is only by God's self-revelation alone that we know truth:

> Long ago, at many times and in many ways, God spoke to our fathers by the prophets, but in these last days *he has spoken to us by his Son*, whom he appointed the heir of all things, through whom also he created the world. *He is the radiance of the glory of God and the exact imprint of his nature.*[71]

That is a truth claim, and it is exclusive by nature. Christians believe that God revealed himself in Jesus Christ, the God-Man. But when the pluralist says, "No one can know if their way is right or wrong," he or she is *also* making a truth claim: "God is not a revealer by nature. No one can know. I am right about this and you are wrong." And that truth claim is also *exclusive by nature*.

Every time you hear someone who is upset because Christianity's claims are exclusive, ask what *that person* thinks is true. And recognize that whatever comes out of his or her mouth is equally exclusive. Every truth claim is exclusive by nature. Period. Even the claim that "no one can know."

Exclusivity: Answers for the Heart

A respectful conversation that involves some kind of House on Fire illustration or a discussion of the Pluralist Paradox can often get the attention of even a committed religious pluralist. But be forewarned. Winning a "head" argument will not win anyone to Christ. The cultural antibody I talked about passes through the head and settles deep within the heart. It produces a toxic soup of fears:

- Fears of self-image: having to acknowledge that for your entire life you have been fundamentally wrong about the most important questions of existence.
- Fears of reputation: the potential of being seen by others as having joined a blatantly exclusive group, as having become a kind of half-crazy fundamentalist.
- Fears of the unknown: not knowing what faith in Christ might mean for one's lifestyle and future.

For all these reasons, and more, it is vital we provide ways for the heart to overcome fear.

Love Overcomes Fear

I have alluded to this already, but the best antidote to the natural fears of the religious pluralist is for the gospel to penetrate deep enough inside of *you* to produce humility, not haughtiness. The apostle Peter put it like this: "in your hearts honor Christ the Lord as holy, always being prepared to make a defense to anyone who asks you for a reason for the hope that is in you; yet do it with gentleness and respect."[72]

I have met many pluralists smarter than me; apologetics is not a battle of wits. I have met many pluralists more moral than I am; it is not a matter of who is the "better person." Any kind of showdown like that is a lose-lose proposition. If I care about people, no matter who they are, I must be humble, gentle, and respectful as I talk with them. It is not only appropriate; it is essential.

Remember, in Christianity I do not get "in" because I am particularly good. I get "in" because I am particularly bad—and because I particularly need a Savior. I have a sin dilemma and I need a sin remedy through the only Person qualified and competent enough to be my Savior. The man who was perhaps the greatest apologist of all, the apostle Paul, always kept this in mind. He wrote, "The saying is trustworthy and deserving of full acceptance, that Christ Jesus came into the world to save sinners, of whom I am the foremost."[73]

If Paul preaches the gospel as the foremost of sinners, what does that imply for you and me? I have taken a cue from Paul. When a pluralist argues that all good people will make it to heaven, my response is always, "Okay, but what about us bad people? You say good people are going to make it to heaven—good Hindus, good Buddhists, good Christians. What about those of us who are bad?" Then they say, "Well, you're not bad; you're a minister!"

And I say, "You don't know my heart."

I have learned the hard way — if I do not approach unbelievers in the attitude of an unworthy sinner saved by pure grace, I merely add fuel to their fears. The heart will never be penetrated with Good News through my efforts alone.

Five Monumental Words

Every religion has a built-in salvation system — a way to get from where you are to where you need to end up, whether it is Nirvana or self-actualization or heaven. The Christian salvation system works on five monumental words, and of those five, four appear in almost every religion. A good way to approach pluralists who have open minds but fearful hearts is to discuss those four words and point out the differences, if any, between the definitions provided by Christianity and other religions. The fifth word *only* shows up in Christianity, and that makes the biggest difference of all.

1. Sin. Virtually every religion says something is wrong with human beings. Something deep down inside of us is broken — so broken that all people in all cultures feel like they are not what they should be, like they do not live up to the standard. They do things that make them feel guilt and shame. Christianity is no exception. It says, "All have sinned."[74]

2. Justice. Virtually every religion believes the world is in a precarious state of balance. When somebody does something wrong, it throws the world out of whack, and something must be done to put it back in order. In

Hinduism it is called karma. Karma is a giant justice system—what goes around comes around. Every action has an equal and opposite reaction. In Christianity, we believe that God is holy and righteous and altogether just. And the world is governed by God's ultimate justice system—all wrongs will be righted, whether in time or eternity.

3. Love. This is where Christianity begins to shine and separate from other religions. Every religion talks about love, but Christianity talks about a different kind of love. Christianity talks about a God who loves you *while you're still a mess*. The essence of Romans 5:8 is that even though we were (and still are) messed-up sinners, God showers us with his love. He doesn't say, "Fix yourself first, and when you're good enough I will welcome you." Instead, he says, "I love you—come to me just as you are." Unbelievable! No other religion talks about God loving us that way.

4. Sacrifice. Every religion talks about sacrifice, but every other religion talks about the sacrifice *you* must make in order to appease God. Only Christianity talks about the sacrifice *God* made to reconcile you to himself. That is a huge distinction. The apostle Peter wrote, "Christ also suffered once for sins, the righteous for the unrighteous, that he might bring us to God."[75]

5. Grace. No other religion talks about grace. It is unique to Christianity. Grace is a culmination of all four of the other words. Grace happens because God loved you so much (and while you were still messed up) that he made a sacrifice so deep it could appease *his* own sense of perfect justice and forgive *your* sin. He offers all of that to you in the form of grace—as a gift you cannot possibly earn or deserve. "For by grace you have been saved through faith, and this is not your own doing; it is the gift of God, not a result of works, so that no one may boast."[76]

Believers who correctly understand and apply the Christian salvation system will never feel superior toward those who subscribe to other religions, or even toward avowed atheists. Why? Because we are not saved or united to God due to any goodness or merit in us—we are saved while we are *bad* because God is gracious. And that makes all the difference in the world. In our system, we are saved by grace. This means when I look at my Hindu neighbor it can be possible for me to admit he is a better person than I am, even as I move toward him with the Good News.

This approach—the true Christian approach of the Bible—can sever the root of the pluralist's fears.

How Far Can You Swim?

Here is another way to say it—another way to break through to the heart. Suppose a person could make it to heaven by swimming across the Atlantic Ocean from New York City to Lisbon, Portugal. It is a distance of 3,000 miles. Let's pretend a person's level of goodness determines the distance he or she can swim.

Jesus said that in order to reach God by yourself, you have to be perfect. So in our analogy, you would have to swim the whole distance—all 3,000 miles. He said, "be perfect, as your heavenly Father is perfect."[77]

Let's start with Mother Teresa, a person who did

incredibly good things. But Mother Teresa included herself when she said, "Jesus died on the Cross because that is what it took for him to do good to *us*—to save *us* from *our* selfishness and sin."[78] So by her own admission, Mother Teresa also falls short in our analogy. Not even she could swim the whole 3,000 miles.

Let's say I am a lousy swimmer and I swim about 100 yards before I begin to flail around and need a savior. You get the point. No one makes it to Lisbon by swimming all 3,000 miles. No one. And no one makes it to God on his or her own "goodness."

We all need a Savior.

If the distance between God's holy perfection and our sinfulness were a mere 3,000 miles, that would be one thing. Maybe someday somebody could swim it. But the distance between us and God's holiness is more like the width of a galaxy. Our need for a Savior is a desperate need. And in that sense, we are all effectively equal. We all fall short.

That's why Christianity is the only religion where I can look at my neighbor and say, "You know what? You are a much better person than I am. But, dear friend, I want you to know you're not going to make it! You can't make it all the way to God on your own. But I have good news. There is a Savior who loves you so much that while you're still flailing around, he has made a sacrifice for you that was so great that it appeased his sense of justice. He offers to forgive your sin. And he offers it to you by way of grace."

Here's the thing: Christianity, in its *exclusivity*, is the most *inclusive* religion the world has ever seen. No other religion in the world is like it. Through the sacrifice of

Jesus, Christianity speaks of grace to those who are good *and* to those who are bad, to those who can swim 200 miles *and* to those who can only make it 100 yards. Even to those who cannot swim at all.

Everybody needs a Savior, and Christianity offers him to us all.

A Final Word on Helping the Pluralist

When you find yourself in a conversation with a pluralist, don't just walk away because you are afraid of the attitudes, or the accusations, or the arrogance, or the scorn. Love more than that. As Christians, we *do* have an exclusive and universal truth. But this should *never* make us feel superior. It should never fill us with pride. Instead, it should enable us to love people from other cultures and other religions like no one has ever loved them before.

Remember: all truth claims are exclusive by nature, so theirs are too. You are on even ground. Then compare the salvation systems of the "many ways" and point out why there is nothing like Christianity.

The world has never seen a belief system this glorious, this wonderful.

* * *

Suppose God enables you to help someone overcome his or her pluralist objections. One big question remains. How can that person be sure the claims of Jesus are true? We will cover that question in our final chapter.

Six

IS JESUS FOR REAL?

Nearly everyone who has studied him will agree: Jesus is a remarkable character. Around 2,000 years ago he was born to a poor family in an obscure village in one of the tiniest countries in the world. He grew up learning a carpenter's trade and never traveled much more than a hundred miles from his birthplace. He never wrote a book. He lived to be just thirty-three years old, and only during the last three years of his life did he gain any public recognition. Yet people everywhere still remember him, marvel at his words and deeds, and fix the Western calendar to the time of his birth.

When the novelist and historian H.G. Wells was asked, "Who was the greatest person in history?" he responded by saying, "I am an historian, I am not a believer, but I must confess as an historian that this penniless preacher from Nazareth is irrevocably the very center of history. Jesus Christ is easily the most dominant figure in all history."[79] Another historian, Kenneth Scott LaTourette wrote, "As the centuries pass, the evidence is accumulating that, measured by his effect on history, Jesus is the most influential life ever lived on this planet."[80]

History's Most Influential Life

Consider the many and varied ways in which our world has been shaped by the example or the teachings of Jesus.

Institutions of compassion. Jesus taught compassion for the down-and-out, for the outcasts, and for the poor. So all over the world you will find orphanages, famine relief centers, and homeless shelters set up and staffed by followers of Jesus.

Jesus also healed the sick and the infirm. So all over the world you will find hospitals set up and staffed by followers of Jesus—people trying to do what Jesus did by taking care of those who hurt.

Personal responsibility. The early followers of Jesus rejected laziness and emphasized the sanctity of labor and the need to work "heartily, as for the Lord."[81] This work ethic has radically boosted the economies of every nation influenced by Christianity.

Business. The teachings of Jesus formed the basis for what has become standard Western business ethics (however imperfectly they are sometimes practiced). And even today, more and more businesses benefit from applying the "Golden Rule" to how they treat their employees and customers.

Social reform. The initiatives that produced the first child labor laws were headed by followers of Jesus. The end of slavery in the British Empire was largely due to the efforts of William Wilberforce, who responded to that injustice based on his understanding of true Christianity. This reform by the British Empire then led to the movement in the Americas to end slavery.[82]

Science. Many of the world's greatest scientists were followers of Jesus: Galileo, Kepler, Copernicus, Roger Bacon, Blaise Pascal, and Isaac Newton, to name a few. Their work was energized by their belief that, since God has established an orderly set of physical laws by which creation operates, then true and valuable things can be learned about those laws.

Art. Over the past 2,000 years, no one has influenced artists more than Jesus. From Michelangelo, daVinci, and Rembrandt, to Bach, Handel, and Beethoven, to Dante, Raphael, and Milton—the list is almost endless.

The Outrageous Claim of Jesus

Jesus is different from the leaders of every other major religion in almost every way. His lifestyle was completely unlike theirs. For example, he was homeless during his public years, and for the most part he associated with lower class, irreligious people. But what most glaringly sets Jesus apart from all other religious leaders is that he claimed to be God.

- Gandhi, Buddha, Confucius, and Mohammad said that if you followed them, they would show you the way to God. But Jesus simply said, "*I am* the way."[83]
- Other religious leaders essentially say, "Follow me, and I'll show you truth." But Jesus said, "*I am* the truth."[84]

- Other religious leaders say, "Follow me, and I'll show you God." But Jesus said, "I and the Father are one," and, "Whoever has seen me has seen the Father."[85]

Every once in a while I'll meet someone who says, "Well, I don't think Jesus claimed to be God—*his disciples* claimed he was God." That is simply not true. Jesus was abundantly clear about this. In fact, his claim to deity is what got him killed. He was crucified not because he committed a crime but because he made a claim, a claim to be equal to God.[86] Jesus unabashedly declared, "To know me is to know the Father."[87] He claimed that to see him was to see God, to believe in him was to believe in God, to hate him was to hate God, to honor him was to honor God, and to love him was to love God.

In chapter 20 of the Gospel of John, Thomas, one of the twelve disciples, falls on his knees and worships Jesus, and Jesus receives that worship and implies it is totally appropriate. Also, Jesus frequently forgave people's sin. Because sin is against God, no one is allowed to forgive sin except God himself, yet Jesus said he has the authority to forgive sin.[88]

As if the deity of Christ was not hard enough for people to swallow, Jesus took these claims a giant step further. He claimed absolute exclusivity. In John 14:6 Jesus said, "No one comes to the Father except through me." No one means NO ONE. Jesus claimed he was the *only* way to God and to heaven.

These statements seem so outrageous that we must ask ourselves: Is Jesus for real? Religious leaders wanting to be worshiped can claim to be divine, but if they cannot back up their claims, they are exposed as phonies. If Jesus is a phony, he can be safely ignored. But if Jesus is God, we had better hang on his every word for dear life.

Just a Good Teacher? Not an Option

It is common these days to hear people say, "I believe Jesus was a good moral teacher. I just wouldn't go so far as to believe he was God or the Son of God." But Jesus does not leave that option open when he claims to *be God*. He cannot be a good moral teacher on the one hand and a blatant liar about his identity on the other.[89] The two are mutually exclusive.

No one would say that cult leaders who made claims of divinity were great moral teachers. A person who claims to be God can only be one of three things: a megalomaniac liar, a delusional lunatic, or . . . exactly who he says he is.[90] There are no other options. Jesus never wanted to give people the option of seeing him as merely a great moral teacher.

That leads to the question, "Can anyone prove Jesus was who he claimed to be?" What proof do we have that Jesus is for real? I will review five separate categories of proof.

Proof #1: The Glass Slipper

Most of you know the story. Her evil stepmother and stepsisters locked up Cinderella, but her fairy godmother granted her one evening out, so Cinderella went to the ball and danced the night away. At the stroke of midnight, she fled, leaving only a single glass slipper and a broken-hearted prince. He looked at that slipper and thought, "If I could only find the foot that perfectly fits this slipper, I will know I have found the one—my only true love, my princess." It's a great story.

The prophets of the Old Testament created a kind of glass slipper with 60 or more prophesies about the coming Messiah. If any person fulfilled all of them, then he was the One. We covered this in chapter three. According to mathematicians, the chances of somebody fitting this particular glass slipper by accident are impossibly, absurdly tiny.[91]

Is Jesus for real? He is the only one who fits the prophetic glass slipper—and that alone should be proof enough.

Proof #2: The Miracles of Jesus

Jesus said, "If I am not doing the works of my Father, then do not believe me; but if I do them, even though you do not believe me, believe the works, that you may know and understand that the Father is in me and I am in the Father."[92] Essentially he is saying, "Watch what I do and you will believe, because only God can do what I do."

Jesus defied the laws of physics and demonstrated absolute authority over the natural world. He turned water into wine, walked on water, calmed a raging storm with two words, gave sight to the blind, healed lepers, raised the dead, and on more than one occasion fed thousands with a few loaves and fishes.

Many people dismiss the miracles of Jesus by saying

the apostles got together and devised a conspiracy of lies. But did you know there were secular historians from Jesus' era who also wrote of his miracles? For example, a Jewish historian named Josephus called Jesus "a miracle worker and a worker of wonders."[93] And Tacitus, a Roman historian, did the same thing and added that when Jesus was transferred from Pilate's custody to Herod's the night before his crucifixion, Herod fully expected Jesus to perform miracles because even he had heard about them.[94]

And even after more than 2,000 years, the miracles have yet to be exposed as frauds. That is why today, if you ask people on the street what Jesus was known for, the vast majority of the time you will hear two things: his teachings and his miracles.

Is Jesus for real? He would answer that question this way: "Even if you don't believe me, look at the miracles, look at what I've done, look at what I was known for, and know that *only God* can do these things."

Proof #3: Jesus, the Standard for Human Behavior

If you walk up to your neighbor and say, "I just want you to know that over the last few weeks, the way you've been acting reminds me of Jesus," even people who don't believe in God recognize that as a compliment. Nobody would take offense, because Jesus' character emerges from the sweep of human history as the highest standard for human behavior. To tell anyone that he or she acts like Jesus is the greatest of accolades, and it has been that way for 2,000 years.

But how can we know that the characterizations we have of Jesus are reliable? We have the stories his closest friends told.

When you get to know people well, you start to see their character defects. A man and woman get married, and before long they see one another as they really are, faults and all. We even have a phrase for it: "the honeymoon is over." Jesus was never married, but he spent three full years with his disciples—especially Peter and John, the closest of the disciples. Surely they would know the real Jesus. So what did Peter say about Jesus' character? He wrote, "He committed no sin."[95] And John wrote, "in him there is no sin."[96] They did not say, "Yes, Jesus was a great guy, a really good teacher." Instead, after "the honeymoon" ended, they said, "When we think back on Jesus, we recognize his absolute perfection. He did not commit a single sin."

Jesus himself agreed. He said publicly, "I always do what pleases the Father."[97] Then, in John 8:44-46, Jesus challenged his critics: "Can any of you prove me guilty of sin?" Would you have the guts to ask that question of anyone, especially an enemy? If I walked into a room to find my wife, my parents, my brother, my kids, my in-laws, and my closest friends, and said, "Hey, I challenge anyone here to name a single sin of mine," they would laugh at me. Then everybody would start talking at once. But when Jesus asked that question to his critics, they came up empty-handed. They did not know what to say. They ended up calling him a name. They said, "Didn't someone say that you are a Samaritan?" That was a big insult back then. Like second graders saying, "You're a doo-doo head."

Go up to anyone on the street and say, "Describe a situation where it's wrong to act like Jesus. Any situation. Just give me one where acting like Jesus would be wrong." Whether they believe in Jesus or not, they are likely to say something like, "Well, that's a trick question because to be like Jesus is to do what is right."

Jesus claimed to be God, and the closer you look at his character, the more convinced you will be that he was not just a good man; his character is held up as the standard of perfection all over the world. Even 2,000 years later.

Proof #4: The Empty Tomb

Jesus made some predictions of his own. He gathered his disciples together and essentially said: "Listen, we're going to Jerusalem, and this is what's going to happen. I'm going to be arrested, convicted, spit on, flogged, and executed, but on the third day I'm coming back—I'm going to rise from the dead."[98]

His disciples were probably thinking, "We've been around Jesus this whole time, and we can't imagine any crime he could be convicted of." That may be why they didn't take him seriously (besides the fact that they were clueless about what "rise from the dead" meant).[99] So they went into Jerusalem, and sure enough, it happened just like Jesus said. He was arrested, convicted, and executed.

The Jewish authorities also knew about the prediction of the resurrection, so they posted guards to secure the tomb to make sure there would be no foul play.[100] But in spite of their best efforts, on the third day the tomb was empty, the body was gone, and the word was spreading like wildfire that Jesus was alive.

Many people shake their head at this point and say, "I just don't buy it. I don't buy that Jesus rose bodily from the dead." But in order to maintain intellectual integrity, they need to offer a plausible explanation for what really happened that particular weekend. If the Son of God did *not* rise from the dead after paying for the sins of mankind, what accounts for the hundreds of thousands of Christians churches all over the world? How could that have happened if the resurrection of Jesus was a hoax?

Proof #5: The Other Explanations for the Empty Tomb

Those who deny the physical resurrection of Jesus have come up with three possible theories to explain the empty tomb. As we will see, none of these theories holds up.

The stolen body. The first theory is that enemies stole Jesus' body. That was what Mary Magdalene thought when she came to the tomb and found it empty. She went running back to Peter and John and said, "They have taken the Lord out of the tomb, and we do not know where they have laid him."[101] She thought that enemies had taken the body to desecrate it and, by hiding it, to prevent Jesus' followers from making his burial place into a shrine.

But as an explanation for what happened to Jesus' body, this theory makes absolutely no sense. Once the rumor began to spread that Jesus was alive, his enemies would have delighted to produce his body. They would have said, "Oh, you mean *this* risen Lord?" And they would have propped his corpse up outside the city gate for all to see. Christianity would have died right then and there.

The swoon theory. This idea has been around for about 200 years but it was made popular by a best-selling 1965 novel called *The Passover Plot*. The idea is that Jesus wanted to fake his resurrection, so he used a drug that would simulate death. He knew he would be executed, so he got someone to give him the drug at the right time in order to *appear* dead before he really *was* dead.

Let's examine what this theory suggests.

We know that Jesus was scourged, which meant he was beaten by professionals so that the bones of his back were exposed. Then they drove nails through his hands and his feet. Later, one of the professional executioners thrust a spear up through his ribcage to make sure he was dead. But according to the "swoon" theory, Jesus had taken his drug and then fooled them by swooning, by playing dead. Then they tore him off the cross, wrapped him in 100 pounds of spices, and put him in a cold, dark, damp tomb where he stayed for three days without food or water. On the third day he woke up from the drug, unwrapped himself, rolled away a two-ton stone, appeared to his disciples, convinced them that he had risen with power and glory, and then went off somewhere else to die. The swoon theory never really caught on because it takes at least as much faith to believe in that as it does to believe in the resurrection.

The conspiracy theory. The final theory is the best. This one came around in the first century, when opponents of Jesus claimed that the disciples stole Jesus' body, reburied it somewhere else, then made up the story of the resurrection and spread the rumor themselves. On the surface, this sounds like a good theory. But all you have to do is dig a little deeper and it completely unravels. I'll explain through a story from my own family tree.

My great uncle Clifton was the last man hanged in Virginia. Seriously. He was not a good man. He killed a few people, so they decided to hang him. He asked for his guitar, sang a song, then turned to his executioners and said, "Listen, you're going to hang me and I'm going to die, but when you take me out of town in that pine box, before you put me in the ground, open it up, because I'm coming back." He promised he was going to resurrect!

So they hanged him and put him in the pine box. When they were taking him away, a spectator who heard him say he was coming back said, "What the heck, let's open it up and see," so they pried the box open and looked inside. What do you think they found? Uncle Clifton, dead as a doornail. The guy looked down at him and said, "Clifton!" No response. So they nailed the box shut again and buried him.

But suppose those guys snuck dead Uncle Clifton out of the pine box, buried him elsewhere, and then told people, "Clifton's up! He's alive—he came back! We saw him!" How long would they continue to spread that false claim if they lost their jobs because of it? Or if they had their kids taken away because of it? Or if they were arrested and brutally beaten and threatened with excruciating death? How many of them would continue to propagate the Clifton Hoax? None.

As I have mentioned, it is an historical fact that nearly every original apostle went to his death for refusing to recant his testimony about Jesus' bodily resurrection. In essence, they said with one accord, "We saw him with our eyes, we touched him with our hands, and Jesus is alive. Kill us if you like, but we will not say otherwise."

Is Jesus for real? A single eyewitness willing to die for his testimony is a compelling witness. Even more if a dozen people concur. Scripture records that at least 500 people witnessed the resurrected Christ,[102] and some significant number of them died for refusing to deny it. Was Jesus for real? Apparently they thought he was. And they were there.

Proof #6: The Testimony of Transformed Lives

Jesus claimed he could transform people's lives. He could fill up what was missing inside of every person. Nicodemus, a very religious man, came to him one night and said, "I have been religious my whole life, but something is missing." Jesus said, "You need to be born again" and told Nicodemus that the connection to being born again—the thing he was missing—was Jesus himself. In essence he told Nicodemus, "Believe in me and everything will come together for you because you will be saved and have eternal life."[103]

In Samaria, a woman came to him at the village well.[104] She had been looking for love in all the wrong places and had felt thirsty her whole life. Jesus said, "The thing you are missing is me. If you ask me, I will become living water inside of you. I will fill the deepest recesses of your soul and you will change, transformed from a miserable woman to a woman filled with joy and purpose."

Over the course of 2,000 years, millions of people have said, "That's exactly what happened to me—Jesus promised to transform me and fill that gap in my heart and connect me with a holy God, and he did. It happened, just as he promised."

Harry Ironside was a pastor back in the 1900s who often preached in open-air assemblies. The broad outlines of a true story about him go like this. One day he was preaching in the street when a man in the crowd, also a well-known speaker, challenged him to debate Agnosticism vs. Christianity. Dr. Ironside said, "Okay, but one condition—you bring one prostitute and one alcoholic who have been transformed by the power of your philosophy, and I will bring 50 ex-prostitutes and 50 ex-alcoholics who have been transformed by the power of Jesus Christ. Then we'll debate." The debate never happened.[105]

In the history of the world, no person even comes close to matching Jesus Christ in the number of people who would testify, "He is the reason I have been transformed."

Indeed, I am convinced that Jesus is for real not just because of proofs but because Jesus transformed *me*. He did in my life exactly what he said he could do—he forgave me of my sins and connected me with a holy God. He gave me purpose and joy and real life. And that is the greatest proof of all. While that's all the proof I need, it's not all the proof I have.

* * *

I believe that in the beginning God created the heavens and the earth, out of nothing. And I believe God created all life. I believe that the Bible is accurate. And I believe that Jesus is the Son of God who takes away the sin of the world. I think the vast majority of the scientific and historical evidence supports those claims. Contrary to what Mr. Kristof wrote in the *New York Times*, I don't believe we have to take our brains and put them on a shelf in order to believe such things. Instead our hearts *and* our brains help us to see that God really does exist, the Bible really is true, and Jesus really is who he said he is.

An Epilogue for Non-Christians: Overcoming Obstacles to Faith

Why don't people believe in Christ? I think you can narrow it down to two basic reasons: pain and power.

Pain and Power

Pain. Many of us have experienced severe pain. Pain that hangs on, defying the adage that time heals all wounds. It might be our own pain or the pain of someone we love. It might simply be the pain of an unjust world. Someone dares to mention God and you ask, "Are you kidding me? If this is the way God treats people, I want nothing to do with him." Against some powerful evidence, we raise our fist and say, "I refuse to believe!" I say "we" because I've been there—for a couple years after my little brother, John, was killed on that motorcycle. We covered the issue of suffering and pain back in chapter four.

Power. But then there is power. Maybe that is your obstacle. This subject goes back to chapter one where we covered The Four Questions of Existence. The point there was that the answers to the first two questions ("Where did I come from?" and "Where am I going?") link directly to the answer to the fourth question ("How shall I live?"). It scares or offends some people to realize that how they live ought to be controlled by how they answer those first two questions. Maybe you feel that way. Maybe you are saying, "You know what? I like deciding how I'm going to live. I like the power of being my own boss. Therefore, I will answer the first two questions in a way that excludes God. That way I can refuse to believe in anything more powerful than myself, and live my life the way I want to."

If there *is* a God, and the Bible *is* true, and Jesus *is* for real, that is a very risky approach to take to life. Please reconsider.

"Do" vs. "Done"

Let's assume you are ready to remove the obstacles of pain and power. Let's say you want to move toward a life of faith in God, but you don't know which religion is for you. I would like to share one more big difference between Christianity and other religions.

Do. Every religion other than Christianity can be summed up with a single word. It's the tiny word "do." If you *do* this, then God will accept you. If you pray five times a day, or if you give enough money, or if you go to church often enough, if you *do this* rather than *that*, then God will probably accept you. I often ask people the question: "If you were to die today and stand before God and he asked why he should let you into his heaven, what would you say to him?" If you would start your answer by saying, "Well, I've tried to do my best, and I didn't do a lot of bad stuff, so my good deeds should outweigh my bad deeds," then you are under the "do" category. That is not the Jesus category.

Done. Christianity can also be summed up by a single word. It's the word "done." Jesus essentially says, "I have *done* something for you—I have died on a cross for your sins. *For your sins.*"

When he was still on that cross, just before he died, he shouted out, "It is finished." What was finished? His work of redemption—the payment of the price of our sins. He had finished paying for it and it was paid-in-full—it was finished, it was done! That is why he offers forgiveness that doesn't have to be earned or deserved. It is a gift made possible by what *he has done*.

If you've felt something missing deep down or know that you have never quite connected to God, then this is the thing you lack—you are missing out on what Jesus has done. The Bible gives step-by-step instructions on how to receive this gift from Jesus. It's not by anything you do, but it is *by his grace*. Here is how you receive that grace:

- Admit you are a sinner, and that you need Jesus as your Savior.
- Recognize Jesus as God's Son who came to substitute himself for you, to pay the price for your sin. Ask him to forgive you based on his finished work on the cross.
- Ask for his love to transform you and the way you approach God from now on.
- Commit your life to Jesus. Acknowledge him as Lord of your life.

As you consider these statements, simply speak to God whole-heartedly and humbly. You do not need incantations or fancy words.

But what if you don't feel ready yet? Then ask God to draw you to himself; ask him to make you ready. In the

Bible, God promises: "You will seek me and you will find me, when you seek for me with all your heart."[106] When that happens, when you really do seek him with your whole heart, something will change qualitatively within you. The process of transformation, becoming the person you were made to be, can then begin.[107]

That is what happens. God promises it, and it happened to me. That is ultimately why I believe Jesus is real.

An Epilogue for Christians: A Final Word for the Apologist

If you are already a Christian, you have probably read this book with a friend in mind. That's great. My hope is that the information in this book will help you share your faith in an effective way with your friend. Let me leave you with three final thoughts.

Never Stray from the Gospel

The two most important words for apologists are *the gospel*. Do not forget you are sharing good news. The good news tells us that even though you are more deeply flawed than you have ever wanted to admit to anyone—even yourself—at the same time you are more deeply loved than you have ever dared to dream. That good news is made possible by the person of Jesus Christ, who lived the life we should have lived and died the death for sin we should have died, so that we can be made acceptable to a holy God, adopted into his family forever.[108]

It is easy to get into discussions with friends and, in a quest to be right about some particular point, lose sight of the gospel. No one was ever won to Christ through that kind of argument. You did not become a Christian because you were smart or right, or because someone who explained the gospel to you was smart or right. You were saved and are saved because you needed a Savior and he came for you—just because he chose to. That is what grace means. Do not lose sight of grace when you share your faith.

Pray

Secondly, do not forget to pray. You are not the most important part of the equation: God's Spirit is. Pray for your friend. Pray for a spirit of wisdom. Pray for God's great love to come shining through. Pray.

Glorify God

Finally, remember that all of this is about God's glory. God is absolutely magnificent, and his Son, Jesus, is spectacular. When in doubt, talk about the Father and the Son. Tell your friends what God has done for you. Tell them why you love him so. God's glory is absolutely astounding. Every human being who sees just a glimpse of his glory will fall to his or her knees in worship. Don't forget that.

May God use you to reflect his glory as you share the truth of the good news of Jesus Christ.

Endnotes

1. Nicholas D. Kristof, "Believe It, Or Not," *The New York Times*, August 15, 2003
2. Matthew 7:24-27
3. Luke 16:19-31
4. I am grateful to Ravi Zacharias for including this idea in one of his messages.
5. Ecclesiastes 3:11
6. Jacqueline L. Salmon, "Most Americans Believe in Higher Power, Poll Finds," *The Washington Post*, June 24, 2008
7. Patrick Glynn, *God: The Evidence* (Roseville, CA: Prima Publishing, 1999), 82-83
8. C. S. Lewis, *Mere Christianity* (San Francisco: HarperCollins, 1972)
9. Glynn, *op cit.*, 61
10. Harold G. Koenig, Michael E. McCullough, and David B. Larson, *Handbook of Religion and Health* (NYC: Oxford U. Press, 2001)
11. Romans 1:20, NIV
12. Stephen J. Gould, *The Panda's Thumb* (New York: Norton, 1980)
13. Hugh Ross, *A Beginner's-and-Expert's Guide to the Big Bang* (Facts for Faith, 2001), 14-32
14. Arno Penzias and Robert Wilson, "Temperature at 4080 Mc/s" as cited in Hugh Ross, *The Fingerprint of God* (Orange CA: Promise Publishing Co., 1991), p 85
15. Ross, *The Fingerprint of God*, p 185
16. R. Douglas Geivett and Gary R. Habermas, eds., *In Defense of Miracles* (Downer's Grove, IL: InterVarsity Press, 1997), 157
17. Colossians 1:7b
18. Hebrews 1:3b
19. Michael Denton, Evolution: *A Theory in Crisis*, 3rd ed. (Chevy Chase, MD: Adler and Adler, 1986), 328
20. William Dembski, Intelligent Design: *The Bridge Between Science & Theology* (Downers Grove, IL: InterVarsity Press, 2002), 10, 107
21. David Foster, *The Philosophical Scientists* (New York: Barnes & Noble Books, 1993), 83
22. Lane P. Lester and Raymond G. Bohlin, *The Natural Limits to Biological Change*, 2nd ed. (Plano TX: Probe Books, 1999), 84-85

23. See, e.g., wiki.answers.com/Q/How_many_atoms_are_there_in_ the_universe and http://en.wikipedia.org/wiki/Shannon_number

24. Charles Darwin, *On the Origin of Species* (Cambridge, MA: Harvard University Press, 1964), 280

25. Gould, *op. cit.*, 181

26. See 1Timothy 3:16. Also note that the Old Testament uses expressions such as "thus saith the Lord" more than 2,600 times.

27. These two manuscripts are known as the Chester Beatty Papyri and the Codex Vaticanus.

28. Lee Strobel, *The Case for Christ* (Grand Rapids, MI: Zondervan, 1998), 63

29. Frederic Kenyon, *The Bible and Archeology* (New York: Harper and Row, 1940), 288-289

30. Michael Martin, *The Case Against Christianity* (Philadelphia: Temple University Press, 1991), 49

31. Luke 1:1-3

32. 2 Peter 1:16

33. 1 John 1:1-3a

34. Acts 2:22

35. Acts 26:26

36. Norman L. Geisler, *Baker Encyclopedia of Christian Apologetics* (Grand Rapids, MI: Baker, 2000), 47

37. Norman L. Geisler and Thomas Howe, *When Critics Ask* (Wheaton, IL: Victor, 1992), 385

38. Simon Greenleaf, *An Examination of the Testimony of the Four Evangelists by the Rules of Evidence Administered in the Courts of Justice*, 1874

39. Matthew 4:4

40. Deuteronomy 8:3

41. Mark 7:13

42. The point here is not that Christianity is the only major religion that has detailed prophecies (some of which are in the Old Testament, and some in the New Testament). In a sense, what I'm saying is stronger—where other religions (such as Judaism) have detailed prophecies, they come from the books of the Old Testament!

43. Henry M. Morris, *Many Infallible Proofs* (Green Forest, AR: Master Books, 1974), 188

44. Isaiah 7:14; cf. Matthew 1:18-25

45. Genesis 12:2, 22:18; cf. Matthew 1:1 and Galatians 3:16

46. Genesis 21:12; cf. Matthew 1:2 and Luke 3:34

47. Genesis 49:10; cf. Luke 3:33 and Hebrews 7:14

48. 2 Samuel 7:12; cf. Matthew 1:1

49. Micah 5:2; cf. Matthew 2:1 and Luke 2:4-7

50. Isaiah 35:5-6; cf. Matthew 9:35

51. Malachi 3:1; cf. Matthew 21:12

52. Psalm 118:22 and Isaiah 53:3; cf. John 1:10-11, 7:5, 7:48, and 1 Peter 2:7

53. Isaiah 53:7; cf. Matthew 27:12-14

54. Psalm 22:16; cf. Luke 23:33

55. Psalm 22:18; cf. John 19:23-24

56. Isaiah 53:12; cf. Matthew 27:38

57. Isaiah 53:12; cf. Luke 23:34

58. Zechariah 12:10; cf. John 19:34

59. Isaiah 53:9; cf. Matthew 27:57-60

60. Peter Stoner, *Science Speaks* (Chicago: Moody Press, 1969), 109

61. Romans 10:9

62. Psalm 62:11-12a

63. Job 1:8

64. Job 2:9

65. Job 42:7-8

66. Isaiah 55:8-9

67. John 11:35.

68. Hebrews 12:2a

69. John 14:6

70. See Matthew 10:5-39

71. Hebrews 1:1-3a

72. 1 Peter 3:15-16

73. 1 Timothy 1:15

74. Romans 3:23

75. 1 Peter 3:18a

76. Ephesians 2:8-9

77. Matthew 5:48

78. Mother Teresa, "Whatever You Did Unto One of the Least, You Did Unto Me" (National Prayer Breakfast, Washington, DC, February 3, 1994), emphasis added.

79. Finest Quotes, http://www.finestquotes.com/author_quotes-author-H.G.%20Wells-page-0.htm

80. Kenneth LaTourette, "The Christian Understanding of History," *The American Historical Review* 54. 2 (January 1949), 259-276

81. Colossians 3:23

82. Eric Metaxas, *Amazing Grace: William Wilberforce and the Heroic Campaign to End Slavery* (Harper One, 2007)

83. John 14:6

84. *Ibid.*

85. John 10:30, 14:9

86. John 5:17-18, 10:30-33

87. See John 14:7

88. Luke 5:24

89. Lewis, *Mere Christianity*

90. *Ibid.*

91. Stoner, *op cit.*

92. John 10:37-38

93. Josh McDowell, *Evidence That Demands a Verdict* (San Bernardino CA: Campus Crusade for Christ, 1972), 85

94. McDowell, *ibid.*, p 84

95. 1 Peter 2:22

96. 1 John 3:5

97. See John 8:29

98. Luke 9:22, 18:31-33

99. Luke 18:34

100. Matthew 27:62-66

101. John 20:1-2

102. 1 Corinthians 15:5-8

103. See John 3:1-21

104. See John 4:1-44

105. E. Schuyler English, *Ordained of the Lord: A Biography of Harry Ironside* (Loizeaux Brothers, 1976)

106. Jeremiah 29:13

107. 2 Corinthians 3:18, 5:17

108. I am grateful to Tim Keller for providing these carefully chosen words to communicate the gospel succinctly.

ABOUT CRUCIFORM PRESS

What would a book-publishing company for gospel-centered Christians look like if it began with the realities of 21st century technology?

We think It would focus on Content, Simplicity, Reliability, Trust, Convenience, Voice, and Community. Here's what we mean by that. These are our promises to you.

Content: Every book will be helpful, inspiring, biblical, and gospel-focused.

Simplicity: Every book will be short, clear, well-written, well-edited, and accessible.

Reliability: <u>A new book will be released the first day of each month. Every book will be the same price.</u> Each book will have a unique cover, yet all our books will maintain a distinctive, recognizable look.

Trust: If you like this book, then you're probably a lot like us in how you think, what you believe, and how you see the world. That means you can trust us to give you only the good stuff.

Convenience: <u>Our books will be available in print, in a variety of ebook formats, and frequently as audiobooks. Print or ebook subscription opportunities can save you time and money.</u>

Voice: We would like to hear anything constructive you'd care to say about what we're doing and how we're doing it.

Community: We want to encourage and facilitate the sense of community that naturally exists among Christians who love the gospel of grace.

Other titles from Cruciform Press
A new book the first day of every month

CruciformPress.com

Made in the USA
Monee, IL
15 November 2020

47810135R00066